Voices of Hope

One Rape Survivor

Plus

Her Family & Friends

Share Their Empowering Road to Recovery

Kristine Irwin

VOICES OF HOPE
ONE RAPE SURVIVOR PLUS HER FAMILY & FRIENDS
SHARE THEIR EMPOWERING ROAD TO RECOVERY

Copyright © 2018 by Kristine Irwin

To contact Kristine:

Website ....: www.voices-of-hope.org

Email.............: Kristine@voices-of-hope.org

LinkedIn ....: https://www.linkedin.com/in/kristine-irwin-mba-b1541267/

Blog...............: https://voicesofhope15.wordpress.com

Facebook ......: https://www.facebook.com/voicesofhope2015/

Twitter..........: https://twitter.com/VoicesofHope15

To contact the publisher, inCredible Messages Press, visit www.inCredibleMessages.com

Printed in the United States of America

ISBN 978-0-9976056-5-5 paperback

ISBN 978-0-9976056-6-2 eBook

Book Coach ....: Bonnie Budzowski

Cover design ....: Bobbie Fratangelo

Author's Photographer ....: Archie Carpenter

Dedication

THIS BOOK IS DEDICATED to my son, Jay, and daughter, Zella. I hope you can experience a world where survivors are believed and loved.

$\mathcal{A}$cknowledgements

THIS BOOK WOULD NOT BE POSSIBLE without the continued support of the family and friends around me. So, for this I thank all of you. I have to start with my loving and supportive husband. If it wasn't for JR, I would not be where I am and who I am today. He is my rock and I know that without him, I would not be able to share my story, not only in this format, but in others. You are my best friend, an amazing father, and my soulmate. Thank you for continuing to fight by my side in hopes of changing our culture, and helping us all gain an understanding.

To my parents, Gary and Tina, I know the road has been long and hard for both of you since 2004. With your support for my healing, and your assistance in helping others to heal from their traumatic experiences, I am able to do what I do. I love you both very much.

To everyone else that I approached about this project and who contributed: Julie, Jenna, Brandon, Izeke, Erin, Courtney, Brenda, Melinda (JR's mom), Jim (JR's dad), and Chris. I know you all were affected in some way by what happened to me. I appreciate you being open to sharing your story about what you went through as a repercussion of what happened to me. I hope that your sharing was a healing process for you. I cannot put into words how thankful I am to have you all by my side.

To everyone else I reached out to but whose story was not included, thank you. Thank you for being there for me and supporting this project. The fact that your words didn't make it in the final edit doesn't mean that your story isn't important. You each have played an important role in helping me heal in some way, and you might not even realize it.

To Bonnie Budzowski and Beth Caldwell, I want to thank you for your help in this journey—from the beginning stages of my idea, to helping me bring it to life, to the final product. I truly can't thank you both enough for all of your guidance and assistance during this process. You have made a process that was part of my healing and difficult for me, at times, a much smoother process, especially with your continued support.

To anyone that has experienced sexual abuse, sexual violence, or domestic violence: I have met some incredible survivors along my healing journey, and you all are simply amazing. I know there are millions more out there that I haven't met. I hope each of you is able to reclaim your life and find the seeds of a fighter that are within you. Know that you are loved and believed no matter what.

It honestly was very difficult to put into words to everyone what you mean to me. You all have been a part of my healing process, and I was able to get where I am because of you.

"We don't heal in isolation, but in community."

– S. Kelley Harrell

Contents

FOREWORD

"I'VE NEVER TOLD ANYONE UNTIL NOW," my friend said, quietly, as we sat across from each other, drinking coffee. "It's been 15 years, and I've never told anyone until now." As a heaviness settled into my chest and tears welled up in my eyes, I blinked and briefly looked away, wishing I could be stronger for my friend as she recalled some of the details of her darkest night. Should I give her a hug? Or say something encouraging? Or cry? Or be angry? Or buy her a helpful book? Simply sitting and listening and absorbing the pain caused by her sexual assault was almost more than I could bear. There must be something we can DO, I thought, or some way to right this terrible wrong.

I could see, however, from the way my friend sat, lost in thought, that what she needed most from me was to simply be there. And, of course, I wanted nothing more than to help her however I could. One thing I hadn't anticipated, though, was how listening to her tell me about her trauma would affect me. I had trouble concentrating, didn't sleep well, felt like I was on an emotional roller coaster, and hated feeling so helpless. Years later, as a trauma therapist, I could look back and see that what I'd experienced was secondary trauma—trauma that results from being exposed to the traumatic experiences of others. First responders, emergency room doctors and nurses, and hospice workers are a few of the professionals who are at risk of developing secondary trauma. Family and friends of someone who has experienced trauma are also at risk, as they listen to what happened and try to help. But as signs of secondary trauma begin to arise, it can be hard to know what to do or how to find help.

This is what makes Kristine Irwin's book so unusual. Not only does she share her own difficult struggles in order to help others who have been through similarly terrible experiences, she also takes time to shed light on what her family and friends went through in trying to support her. Navigating the "uncharted waters," as Irwin so perceptively observes, of helping someone who has been traumatized can be confusing, to say the least. There is no playbook to help you understand what to say or how to help—or what to do when you begin to buckle under the stress. Where do you turn? Who do you talk to? How do you keep supporting your loved one when your own struggles become too overwhelming?

If you happen to be feeling this way, this book has much to offer to you. Through the many stories and perspectives shared by Kristine Irwin's family and friends, we get a clear picture of the many different ways family and friends are impacted—and sometimes even traumatized—by the traumatic experience of their loved one. Indeed, a traumatic experience doesn't just affect that person; it affects everyone around them—family, friends, neighbors, and communities.

People often ask me how I can bear to do my work. "I just couldn't listen to all of the awful things people must tell you," they say. Over the many years of working as a trauma therapist, I've learned how to listen to the suffering of others and still care for myself in order to lessen the risk of secondary trauma. One of the most enjoyable ways I do this is by focusing on how people transform their pain and suffering into something positive and healing. "Post-traumatic growth" is the clinical term, and witnessing this is one of the most delightful parts of my work! In sharing her experiences with honesty and vulnerability, not only in her book, but also through her non-profit, Voices of Hope, Kristine Irwin is indeed giving all of us the gift of hope. She is helping countless people who have been through sexual assault or abuse to find their own path of hope. And she is helping countless family members, friends, neighbors, and communities to see that they, too, can transform their pain and trauma into something meaningful and purposeful.

The journey you are about to undertake in reading this book is as important as it is poignant. Life is never quite the same after a trauma. And yet, as new green grass arises from wildfire-scorched ground, beauty can arise after tragedy. In reading this book, you become part of a larger community of people working to heal themselves, their loved ones, and their communities. May this book move you, inspire you, comfort you, and, above all, give you hope.

Amy Sugeno, LCSW, Clinical Ecotherapist
Marble Falls, Texas

CHAPTER 1

FROM INNOCENT TO INJURED

THE PERSON WHO CALLED THE AMBULANCE for me was a complete stranger. Over a decade later, I'm still indebted to this woman, and I don't even know her name.

The woman told the police that when she saw a car at a stop sign on her street, she initially thought nothing of it. When the car was still there a few minutes later, the woman began to watch it. Eventually, she watched as the passenger door opened and I spilled onto the ground. The car drove away and left me by the side of the road, covered in mud and leaves. The stranger called 911 and stayed with me until the ambulance came. I remember none of it.

I do remember waking up in the hospital, feeling disoriented and asking a nurse, "What am I doing here?"

Answering, the nurse pulled no punches, "You are here because you were raped."

The crime occurred on October 4, 2004, when I was 19 years old and a freshman in college.

I had come home from college excited to spend time with my crush, whom I'll call Steve. I had met Steve the previous summer while working at a convenience store. For reasons I'll never fully understand, I became obsessed with Steve and fitting in with his group of friends, even though I had great friends of my own. My obsession had led me to make five months' worth of bad decisions, enough that my friends and my parents were worried about the change in me. I'd begun drinking heavily and sneaking around. In spite of repeated warnings and red flags, Steve—and fitting in with his friends—were the only things that mattered to me.

For months, I had been chasing Steve. Looking back, I realize he wasn't particularly into me. But it wasn't Steve who raped me. It was his friend, whom I'll call Karl. This book is the story of how the whole thing happened and what I've learned from the experience. It's also about how my rape affected my family and friends and what we have all learned because of the experience.

I want to tell you my story for a number of reasons. For one thing, telling my story helps me to heal. The rape is a major event in my life, and talking about it is a way to keep the crime from defining me. Although it's been over a decade since the incident, I'm still integrating the experience constructively into my life. Talking reduces its power over me.

I believe we all need to talk more openly about rape. Currently, we have a culture of silence surrounding this topic. The silence has multiple consequences. For starters, perpetrators get away with, and repeat, their crime. Victims suffer in silence and shame, too embarrassed to reach out for the support they deserve. Families of victims also suffer in silence, protecting the privacy of their victimized loved one. In this way, families become isolated when they really need support. This pattern often leads to brokenness and even divorce within the families.

If we do talk openly about rape, we can learn to be realistic about the danger, and take steps to prevent it from happening to us or our friends.

* * * * * *

THE SUMMER OF 2004

I remember it well, at least most of it. I graduated from high school at the end of May in the city of Johnstown, in south-western Pennsylvania. I was excited to have the summer months to spend with my friends before I went off to Point Park College in the city of Pittsburgh, about 70 miles away. I couldn't wait.

The summer started as any typical summer did. I continued to work as a server at Red Lobster, the job I had throughout the school year. I also decided to return part time to a summer job I'd had before, as a cashier at a convenience store, to make some extra money. My schedule was great. I worked both jobs throughout the week and then got to hang out with all of my friends from high school, including Erin, Pinkas, Mark, Chris, Dez, Jenna, and Brandon, just to name a few.

We were a close-knit group, many of whom had known each other for years. In fact, I had known my friend, Pinkas, since kindergarten. My parents had always made our house a comfortable "hang out" place for my friends. My parents knew my friends, and had even served as chaperones on a school trip to Europe. My parents knew many of my friends' parents as well.

I remember having a lot of fun during the first month-and-a-half of summer, and most of the time, our activities didn't involve any alcohol. We knew we didn't need alcohol to have a good time. We spent time together at each others' houses, at a local Denny's, and a billiard joint. Goofing off was enough.

Once I began working at the convenience store, I became friendly with a couple of guys who worked with me. I developed a crush on Steve, and that crush seemed to grow every day. Every time I went to work at the convenience store, I enjoyed the attention I was getting from Steve. Everyone likes a little attention now and then, especially from a young, attractive guy. Karl, and some others in a group of friends with Steve, also worked in the convenience store. The jokes and teasing we shared made our work shifts fun.

One night, the group of guys from the convenience store invited me to party with them at a local cemetery. I agreed to go. My friend, Pinkas, remembers being surprised and somewhat alarmed when I started to go off alone with the group of guys. Pinkas related the story to me like this:

> *I remember one night in June, we were all at the local pool hall, and out of the blue you started to leave. When I asked where you were going, you informed us that you were going to go to a party in Crum Cemetery.*
>
> *When I asked who else was going to be there, you replied, "Oh, just the guys and me."*
>
> *Mark and I were not going to allow you to attend this party by yourself. We invited ourselves and Ann to go along.*
>
> *I remember seeing faces of surprise and confusion when we got out of the vehicle with you at the cemetery. Mark, Ann, and I clearly weren't welcome.*
>
> *I began to worry seriously about you that night. I was infuriated with you—that you wanted to leave our group and go to the backside of the cemetery by yourself to party with four guys. It wasn't safe or smart to put yourself in a situation like that.*
>
> *I would be leaving for the Navy in September, and I wouldn't be around to protect you. I remember telling Mark my concern and telling him he would need to step up more and be more intrusive after I left for the Navy. I did not trust these guys and just had an overall bad feeling about them.*

Looking back, I shiver at the thought of that party and its location far out in the woods. I can't believe I thought a remote cemetery was a good place for a party. Little did I know what would happen in those woods a few months from that night.

The guys clearly weren't happy that I had brought my friends, but I didn't pay much attention to that. Pinkas and Mark were like brothers to me, and I was glad to have them and Ann there. Mostly, I was just excited to hang out with my crush and have my friends meet him. Along with Steve and Karl, a third guy who worked with us was there.

We spent most of the night drinking with them. My high school friends behaved responsibly, and Ann appointed herself our designated driver. When we decided to leave, we went back to my house and stayed there. In my intoxicated state, I proceeded to tell my three friends how much I liked Steve. I was glad they had met Steve, but I wouldn't have cared if they didn't. I was obsessed.

My mind was filled with Steve that summer. I couldn't get enough of him. I remember taking my mom to the convenience store to meet Steve and the other guys. Even so, I didn't invite the guys from the convenience store over to my house the way I frequently invited my high school friends. The definition of a good time differed between the two groups. From that first party at the cemetery, I felt a tension between my high school friends and the convenience store guys. My longtime friends were concerned for me because they saw my personality changing. I was mostly oblivious and didn't care anyway. Something was driving me to Steve.

The summer went by quickly, and at the end of August, my parents packed me up and we drove to Pittsburgh to move me into my new dorm room at Point Park College. My parents moved me in and helped me decorate. My new roommate, Courtney, wasn't coming until the next day.

This was a time of transition for all of us. We had just had to put down our beloved family dog, and my mom was starting a new job that required her to travel more. I remember my dad saying, "I wonder what your roommate is going to say when she sees all your pictures of your dog that passed." I had gotten that dog when I was in second grade, and the loss was fresh. The dog grew up with me, so of course I took pictures. I was concerned that my dad would be alone at home, missing my mom and me, and without even a dog for comfort. I decided right then to find a new puppy for my dad.

Meanwhile, I remember being a bit apprehensive about meeting Courtney, my new roommate, but she was amazing. We clicked from the start. And Courtney wasn't bothered about the dog pictures or my search for a puppy. Looking back, all of us, including my parents, seemed to have such innocent concerns.

College started out great! I had a great roommate, and I loved the newfound freedom. Classes were good, too. I was studying TV broadcasting, with the aspiration of eventually becoming a news anchor. Even so, I didn't fully dig into college social life—because something/someone was always in the back of my mind. Steve. I became even more obsessed over him.

Steve was attending college in Greensburg, roughly 30 miles from Point Park, and 45 miles from Johnstown. I tried to talk to Steve on AOL instant messenger and would try to hang out with him on the weekends. Some weekends we got together, and some we didn't. Steve was mysterious and I was the one "chasing" him; he definitely was not chasing me.

When I met Steve and we began to "hang out," I desperately wanted to fit in with him. He was a partier, so I transformed like a chameleon and attempted to become a partier when I was with him. Until then, I had never been a drinker. I knew people who drank and I had tried alcohol a few times before that summer. That was it.

Now, my drinking began to escalate, even when I wasn't with Steve. Courtney had a connection to get us served in a local bar, and we drank together. Even so, I preferred to spend my weekends at home. I began sneaking home without my parents' knowledge by finding rides from my roommate or even from Steve.

One weekend, I went home to see some of my friends from high school. My parents knew I was in town. We were all hanging out at a local restaurant, when I got a text from Steve about going to a party. Erin has a clear recollection of that night:

> We were hanging out in Johnstown at Denny's and Kevin, Ann, Mark, and I were waiting for you to meet us and go back to my house. You were supposed to stay over, but you were out with those guys from the convenience store. I was frustrated because I thought these guys were shady, but I also knew I did not know them at this point. I was going to give them a chance because you seemed to like them. I also hated them deep down, because they took you away from our group of friends.
>
> We waited and waited until those guys showed up in a car, and they still wouldn't let you out. I became nervous and worried for you. The guys from the convenience store were antagonizing us, and we could all tell that you were very drunk. Our main mission was to get you to us, whatever it took.
>
> I had to call my dad and tell him what was happening because we were all supposed to have been back at my house an hour earlier. My dad was understanding, but worried, too. He asked me to keep him posted.
>
> Ultimately, we dragged you out of that car when those guys finally dropped you off at Denny's. You were very out of it. We got you back to my house, and we were all angry—at you, and especially at those guys.
>
> You were lying on my dining room floor with leaves and puke in your hair. I remember thinking how awful this whole night turned out to be for everyone. I hated seeing you so crazy drunk; it was not a fun drunk. I remember wondering what they did to get you this drunk and to convince you to stay with them and not meet up with us. I thought these guys were devious and conspiring.

> *I had to bathe you that night and put you to sleep. My dad and I woke up nearly every hour to check on you. I was exhausted the next morning, and my dad made us a big breakfast. He was upset for you, and he knew he had to tell your parents about what happened. I always thought that you were mad at me for telling your parents about what happened, but I knew it would be my biggest regret if we didn't tell them.*

I remember that night, but of course, not as well as Erin does. I looked back through some journals and saw what I wrote about that party:

> *The last thing I remember is being somewhere in the woods with a group of my crush's friends. They were passing around a Coke bottle that had hard liquor in it, daring each other to see who would drink it all. I immediately grabbed the bottle out of their hands and chugged it. I finished the whole thing.*

No wonder I was wasted and had puked all over myself. I was falling so hard for this guy who wasn't even worth my time, and I was slowly destroying my life, as well as my relationships with my friends and family. Oh, the things I wish I could say to my younger self.

The day after that party, I remember the drive home to my parents', knowing that they knew I had gotten drunk. I was in high spirits and could care less what my parents thought. I felt I could take whatever they threw at me. I was overconfident. I felt I was invincible, and that nothing bad would ever happen to me. I remember getting home and sitting in front of my dad. He asked me if I felt I was responsible enough to drink, and I responded that I thought I was.

As a consequence of my behavior that night, I was not allowed to use my car when I came home from college to visit. I had to get rides everywhere I needed to go. My dad also delivered a serious lecture to me and Mark, who happened to be visiting that day. Dad told us that friends have to watch out for each other. We have to be there for each other, and not allow either of us to leave alone with anyone. It seems my dad knew what bystander intervention was before I did. He drove the point about safety home as strongly as he could.

My dad's lecture didn't sink in for me. At any rate, I knew Steve and his friends. I wasn't going off with strangers. So, I didn't think twice when Steve picked me up from school on a Friday night to go to a party at his house. Once again, I felt I had to prove myself as a "partier." I don't remember this party night or some of the others, but I never felt like Steve took advantage of me. I'm not sure what his motives were. For my part, I was just trying to fit in with the party crowd and hoping that eventually Steve would like me.

The week of October 4th, I made plans to go home on Friday afternoon without my parents' knowledge. My roommate, Courtney, was going to drive me to her home, which was half way between my hometown and school. Then Steve was going to drive me to my friend Chris's house in my hometown.

THE INCIDENT

I was so excited to ride home with Steve, and to have the whole weekend to do whatever I wanted, without my parents' interference. I didn't have a car, so I was limited there, but that wouldn't stop me. I remember asking Steve on the drive home if we would be able to hang out Friday or Saturday night. He played it off that we might be able to get together. I still was hopeful.

Once we arrived in Johnstown, Steve dropped me off at my friend Chris's house. That Saturday, I spent a lot of the day with Mark. We went and saw a movie, and then eventually made it to our favorite pool hall. There, we got to hang out with some other friends.

I was with my friends that evening, but my mind was on Steve, still hoping to see him. When I got a text from Karl, one of Steve's friends who also had worked with us over the summer, asking if I wanted to go to a party where Steve would be, I immediately said, "Yes."

Karl picked me up and the two of us left together. I do not remember asking any of my friends to go with me, nor do I remember any of my friends offering or trying to stop me from going. Once we left, Karl drove to his house and picked up some alcohol. We drove around for a bit, but eventually ended up at Crum's Cemetery, the same cemetery we were at a couple of months ago with Pinkas.

I decided to have a beer, and Karl and I just hung out and talked. We had a friendly conversation, and I was completely comfortable. I remember talking about Steve and saying how much I liked him. Karl told me I shouldn't drink too much around Steve; it actually turns guys away. He talked to me about his girlfriend and asked for some advice regarding her. Karl took a few swigs from a bottle of Crown Royal and asked me if I wanted any. I said, "No," and afterward, he asked several more times. I finally gave in and took a big swig. That is the last thing I remember.

Then I was waking up in the hospital, and asking a nurse why I was there. She looked at me and said, "You are here because you were raped." She also informed me that I had had a rape test kit done, and had been given Plan B to prevent pregnancy. When the nurse told me my parents were on their way, I'm sure she meant to comfort me, but I was miserable. What would they say about me sneaking home and ending up like this? I knew that I was going to disappoint them. All my life, "disappoint" was a trigger word for me; I think it went hand in hand with having limited self-confidence. But I was sure I was a disappointment in that moment.

I don't remember anything about the rape, which is surprising, because rape is such a violent crime. I also don't remember much else from those disoriented hours in the hospital, except that I had an urge to eat. I was pushing the experience down from my consciousness and trying to dull the edges of pain in accordance with the eating disorder, bulimia. I had struggled with bulimia for a number of years and thought I had it licked. The trauma of my situation put me right back into that mode. I needed to eat to suppress my feelings.

My friends Chris and Mark had looked for me all night. The next morning, a paramedic answered my phone as they were treating me in the ambulance. That's how Chris and Mark learned what had happened.

Chris felt like he had failed me because I was supposed to be staying at his house that weekend. He felt he might have been a voice of reason and persuaded me to stay with our group. Mark was enraged, but he was also feeling guilty, because he had been with me at the other end of my dad's lecture on watching out for each other and never letting each other go off alone. Mostly, they were relieved because they had feared the worst when they couldn't find me all night.

I had been drinking a lot in those days, and my friends had been taking care of me. I kept taking risks, and my friends kept rescuing me. I refused to heed their warnings, or the one from my dad. This time, the risk turned into a disaster.

While my friends frantically looked for me, my parents were staying overnight at a local resort called Seven Springs. They had won a weekend there as a prize and invited me, plus a few of my friends, to join them. Hoping to see Steve that weekend, I lied and said I was going to the movies with a friend at school. I did go see a movie that weekend with Mark, but that doesn't mitigate the lie.

I still feel distressed when I imagine my parents, out for a fun weekend, receiving a call from a Richland Township police officer, saying I had been thrown from a vehicle and was in the hospital. My mom tells the story this way:

> I was too upset to take in the news, so I handed the
> phone to my husband, Gary. After a brief conversa-
> tion, Gary hung up. We frantically packed and sped to

the hospital, a 40-minute drive away. I remember us saying to each other, "We don't even know if she's alive."

At the hospital, the officer talked to my husband alone, delivering the news about the rape. The officer told us both about how a woman saw Kristine being dumped on the side of the road and called 911. We learned that the paramedics found Kristine covered in mud and leaves, and that the nurses and doctors had worked on Kristine for hours before they called us.

I was shocked that afternoon when the doctors told us Kristine could be released to go home. I had so many mixed emotions. I was sure of one thing, however. I had never dealt with anything like this before, and I was utterly unprepared. I refused to leave the hospital until they summoned someone who could help us know what to do next.

The hospital staff called Victim Services, and the woman who came was a blessing. She comforted us and promised to be with us every step of the way. Over the next few days and weeks, we would really need her.

CHAPTER 2

SHOCK, GRIEF, AND LEGAL PROCEEDINGS

MY MEMORIES OF THE HOSPITAL ARE FOGGY, but the ride home in the car with my parents is clear. It was the quietest car ride ever. I don't know what my mom and dad were thinking as I stared out the window in silence. For me, the world out there was suddenly a dark and scary place. So much for the innocent perspectives we shared as I was moving into my college dorm just a month earlier.

I walked into the house like a dog with its tail between its legs and headed straight for the living room couch. Feeling tired, weak, and disoriented, I fell asleep. A few hours later, I woke up in a panic. I was frightened and couldn't make out the time on the VCR. I thought it might be the next day and I began to cry.

Mom came in and told me it was only 6 p.m. I asked her if she still loved me, and she said she always would. She said my dad loved me too, but he thought it was my fault and she wasn't sure what to believe. I felt like crap. I didn't even know what to think of myself. Mom also said, "You know, you could get charged with underage drinking." I don't know what I said to that. Mom also said, "Every day will be better than this one. Every day we will move forward."

The next thing I remember is learning that my dad had left the house without telling my mom where he was going. She immediately started calling extended family members to find him. She learned that my dad had gone to my Uncle Dan's house, only to sit outside the door crying. He never even went into the house. Dad must have told someone what happened, and that person called my dad's other brother.

Soon, our house was filled with my aunts and cousins. My dad still wasn't there. Now they all knew my shame. I don't remember talking to them—if I did—or what anyone said. I don't remember anything until the next morning. I think I also called my college roommate that night to let her know what happened and that I wouldn't be back for about a week.

That Monday morning was better than Sunday, but it was not a great day of my life by any means. My dad had apparently come home and had gone to work at his regular time. I was alone with my mom. I got up and decided to shower.

I finally was able to cleanse myself of the weekend's events. I felt okay, except that I finally saw the bruises. I found a bruise on my left breast, one on my inner thigh, another on my arm, and one on my quad. I had been told there was also a bruise on my heel, but I couldn't find it. I walked out of the bathroom to find my mom to show her my bruises. She was on the phone with the police. I let her finish her conversation and then I showed the bruises to her. Neither of us could find the bruise on my heel.

While I was numb and sleeping, protecting myself in a fog at the hospital and that first day at home, my parents' world had been turned upside down. Life had gone from normal to bizarre with the initial phone call my parents had received from the police. Dad describes his initial feelings:

> *It's the call that no parent ever wants to get, to come to the hospital. Driving down to the hospital, your mind is racing a million miles a minute. Once you are there and find out what happened, you are in shock.*

From the time my baby was born, I was responsible to teach and protect my baby, show her right from wrong. When something like this happens, you feel like you failed. You are mad and want to kill the bastard that raped her. You want to understand what you could have done differently to protect your baby.

Dad was angry that Mark and I hadn't heeded the lecture he had recently given us. He just couldn't get over it. If we had stayed together and looked after each other, this crime would have been prevented. Now, his baby was traumatized. Dad not only felt like he had failed me, but that God had failed him in failing to protect me. He says:

I grew up being a religious person and was always trying to live a good life and help others. I tried to be charitable and prayed to God to protect my family. After this happened, I was angry with God and wondered how he could let this happen to my baby. I lost religion over this.

Meanwhile, my mom was trying to hold herself together for all of us. Her personal trauma ranged from not knowing initially if I was even alive, to the shock of rape, to worrying about my dad, to the awkwardness of relatives trying to show their support in uncharted waters. Lost in my own trauma, I had no idea what my parents were going through.

* * * * * *

After looking at my bruises, my mom told me we had to go to the police station for questioning. I dressed in sweatpants and a sweatshirt, always my choice of clothes when sick. Because I wasn't going back to school for a week, I felt as if I were sick. I didn't put on makeup and I didn't care what I looked like.

We left the house, drove to the station, and found a seat in the waiting room. Soon a woman entered and asked if I was Kristine. She introduced herself as an advocate from Victim Services. She had long, brown-blonde hair and was about the same height as I am. She was pretty and seemed nice enough.

The advocate talked to my mom and me about what we were going to do that day. First, I had to give my statement, and write down everything I had done on Saturday leading up to the incident. Then, we were going to drive out to the crime scene.

I have vague memories of feeling confused as I wrote my statement because I couldn't remember a huge chunk of time. I felt as if I was missing the most important part, but I couldn't access it.

Afterward, we drove to the crime scene, that cemetery deep in the woods. There we found two condoms and a garbage bag containing an empty liquor box. Inside that box were my socks and underwear.

It turned out that the crime scene in the cemetery was in a different jurisdiction from Richland Township, where I had been left by the side of the road. After telling my story and collecting evidence on Monday, I had to go and tell the story to different officers on Wednesday. I was scared. The police always scared me, even when I just saw them driving around in their squad cars. Now they wanted me to sit in a police station and calmly tell the worst story of my life for the second time.

Once again, my mom fielded the phone calls and arranged for the woman from Victim Services to meet us. We met at a McDonalds, and that made me think of food. I was resorting once again to my bulimia. While I was distracted by thoughts of food, my advocate was trying to get my attention and ask if I was okay. I said, "I am all right, just nervous about seeing the police again."

She assured me the officer would be nice. Driving from McDonalds to the police station in a tiny town, I stared out the window at the trees and the gray sky. My brain raced with questions and thoughts: "How did I get myself into this? This isn't supposed to happen to me. Bad things aren't supposed to happen to me." But this bad thing had definitely happened.

Mom has a memory that shows just how naïve and confused I was. As part of the agenda that day, I had to be fingerprinted. An officer asked if I had ever been fingerprinted before. Mom answered, "No."

I interrupted to say, "Yes, I have." I was referring to the experience in kindergarten when kids were fingerprinted in case of abduction. The police officer had meant something else entirely.

As the police recorded my statement, my mom, as well as my advocate, was there to support me. My mom, however, had to leave in the middle. The account was just too upsetting.

The burden of caring for me and worrying about my father, as well as dealing with her own feelings, was overwhelming. Here is how my mom describes her state of mind during those first months:

> *The incident happened on a Saturday. It was now Wednesday and I had not gone to work. I could barely function. Gary [my husband] sat on our recently deceased dog's gravesite and cried. I tried to get everyone to go to counseling. Gary didn't think he needed to, but he finally agreed to meet with Victim Services.*
>
> *I took Kristine back to school a week later, and I tried to go back to work. I encouraged Kristine to reach out and work with the counselors at her school. When I returned to work, I only told one person, in addition to my Human Resources representative, what was happening. They encouraged me to take a leave, but I said I wanted to try to stay.*
>
> *The rape consumed my every thought, my every minute. I tried to understand what happened, why us, what we did wrong. I went to a counselor. I told her I felt like I had a baby bird that I had let try to fly and,*

as soon as I let it go, the baby fell and broke its wing.
Now, I was trying to nurse it back to health.

Gary was bitter and I couldn't take the stress and ten-
sion in the household. I finally sat both of them down
and insisted they tell each other that they loved each
other. It was very hard for me. I felt like I was caught
in the middle of this big, ugly story.

My sister-in-law told me that she knew a couple who
went through a similar situation. The couple ended up
divorcing. I was determined that my family would stay
together and that we would become stronger. I just
didn't know how.

At my parents' insistence, I came home from school every week-end for a while. They kept a tight rein on me, but I was allowed to work, so I went back to my part-time job at Red Lobster. I was okay with being grounded, but felt a little caged.

At school, the next few months were crazy. I was in denial, and I began to party more. I still had feelings for my crush for at least a month following the incident. I found out he had gotten a girlfriend, which upset me. I also found out that my crush told someone I had only been interested in him for sex.

I don't know if my crush came to this conclusion because of what happened with his friend, Karl, but it most definitely wasn't the case. I had just wanted Steve's attention and the fantasy of a romance.

While I was partying, struggling, and giving in to my bulimia at school, the district attorney and police officer handling my case were calling my mom every few days. Mom went to work and felt she had to act as if nothing was wrong. She worried about me constantly. It was hard for her to deal with all the stress and stay focused at work, especially because her job in-cluded travelling.

Sometimes my mom thought about my rapist and his family. She wondered if he had just made a mistake. She wanted to know what caused this horrible thing to happen. She felt that seeing where my rapist lived might help her to understand more about him and his family. On her lunch hour one day, my mom drove by Karl's house looking for answers. But there were no answers.

At other times, she thought about how unfair the culture surrounding rape is. After all, if a kid breaks a leg, the mom can talk to everybody about it. If a kid is a victim of rape, the mom keeps quiet and no one knows what she is going through. No one brings a casserole.

One day in early January, the district attorney called my mom to say he had enough evidence to make an arrest. I was summoned to appear in court. I remember sitting in the waiting room. Soon, I saw two garbage bags being carried into a room. I knew this was the evidence, including my clothes and the underwear they found in that liquor box.

Then, I saw my perpetrator and his family. My heart jumped in my throat. It felt as if a big rock were on my chest and I couldn't breathe. Karl didn't look once at me. I looked at him and immediately turned away. I cannot get the image of him walking into the preliminary hearing out of my head. I don't remember exactly what I was thinking, only that I didn't want to be there. I remember that all my friends who had been with me the night before the rape came to the trial to support me. I remember only fragments of the proceedings, not even the outcome.

My mom remembers seeing my perpetrator and his family, and feeling sick, stressed, and emotional. It was hard for my mom to see the perpetrator's mother, knowing how she felt as my mother.

Ultimately, the legal proceedings took two years, but the preliminary hearing was the only hearing I was required to attend. Mom fielded calls from the district attorney all that time, worrying about me and trying to protect me from the trauma of testifying. Eventually, the perpetrator took a plea deal and was put on probation. He didn't suffer the full consequences of the crime he committed, but the legal proceedings were finally over. Eventually, the perpetrator went to prison because of another crime.

CHAPTER 3

Boyfriends, Bad Judgment, and Betrayals

I NEVER EXPECTED TO SAVE MYSELF SEXUALLY for marriage, but I wanted my first time to be with someone I trusted, someone who loved me for *me*. Throughout high school, I knew I was too young for a mature relationship, so I never had sex.

I was a naïve girl who wanted a magical romance, like the ones in the movies. I wanted to be wanted and wooed. My first sexual experience was to be the icing on the cake in a relationship with a Prince Charming who adored me.

When my virginity was stolen by rape, and my innocence shattered, I felt torn and confused. My fantasies about sex were gone, and I didn't know what to think about sex anymore. I was damaged, and I didn't even remember the experience. Far from my romantic dream, my first sexual experience was so violent that I repressed all memory of it. Ten-plus years later, I still don't remember it.

After the rape, I didn't see a reason to wait for sex, but I also didn't have a concept of a healthy sexual relationship. It almost seemed as if sex was something that was "supposed to happen" after I had a few drinks in my system. Sober, I was uncomfortable with my body image, myself, and the fact that I was now damaged goods.

Insecurity and a generalized discomfort with my body wasn't new for me, but it intensified after the rape. The bulimia that was resurfacing now had developed during my sophomore year in high school, shortly after my grandmother died. I remember exactly how it started.

A dancer since age three, I competed in ballet, tap, and jazz until my senior year of high school. At the end of my sophomore year, my grandmother on my mother's side passed away. I remember the day as if it were yesterday. I was sleeping in because we had no school that day, and my dad yelled up to me. When I walked downstairs, he told me my grandmother had passed away. It wasn't a huge surprise, since we had learned a number of months before that she had pancreatic cancer. The doctors had anticipated that she wouldn't have much longer to live, even with chemo.

I remember my dad leaving for work that morning and spending the morning by myself, watching the movie *Lassie* and crying over Lassie, and not my grandmother. I don't remember crying very much during that time, which seemed odd to me, but insecurities about my body began to surface.

One day, I confided to another dancer that I was unhappy with my body. She explained her own strategy: "I eat whatever I want, and then I throw up." I tried it and was soon hooked. The empty cookie boxes my mom found beneath my bed, along with other signs, alerted her to a problem. It took a number of tries before she found someone who would diagnose me properly and begin to help.

From the outside, I must have looked successful in high school. Elected to my school's homecoming court, I also competed in the Outstanding Young Women scholarship program/pageant. On the other hand, when asked during the competition to name one aspect of my life I would change if I could, I answered, "Be more happy."

Looking back on it now, I wish that competition would have been a wakeup call for me. I wish I would have understood that my answer was a sign that I needed help, that I was using the eating disorder to mask depression and couldn't come to terms with the death of my grandmother. But I couldn't know this, because I just threw up all my feelings all the time. I put a lot of pressure on myself to keep everyone happy and not disappoint others.

Happiness and acceptance by others were always mixed together for me. Perhaps that's why I had gone to such extremes to be accepted by my crush's partying friends. Now, after the rape, everything I knew as normal was upset. I had thought I had gotten the bulimia under control, but it was back.

I felt driven to be in a relationship. It was if I had no self-worth unless it came from a man. At one point, Courtney and I joined a dating website. I remember one night, an older man wanted to meet me. I remember going downstairs to the security entrance with Courtney; we ended up asking security for him to leave because we felt it wasn't right. I met another guy through some friends, and he was really nice. We went on a great date together, and he actually was someone I thought I could truly trust. But because of my mental state at the time, the "good guys," the actual "guys I could trust," were a no-go for me, and I broke it off with him by sending Courtney to tell him I didn't want to see him.

I developed a crush on another guy, whom I'll call Charles, as Christmas approached, and I dove headfirst into the relationship. Charles and I met through mutual friends, and most of the time we hung out with all of our friends. Sometimes, of course, Charles and I hung out alone. I remember having sex with Charles one time. It was consensual, but I admit I had a few drinks beforehand at a party. Looking back at that instance, I realize that I would not normally have sex under those circumstances. But I didn't think that way because I had a crush on this person, and this is what it must be like to be in a relationship.

Meanwhile, my dad and I struggled with our own relationship. Because I did not have a car at school and was not allowed to go anywhere alone when I was home, my dad would pick me up from school. One weekend, my dad sat me down and cried.

He said he was worried that I was alone at school and had no one. He at least wanted me to have someone to sit with at lunch. I assured my dad I had someone to sit with at lunch. I wasn't okay, but I had people. I felt horrible dragging my dad down with my emotional mess.

In early January 2005, just three months after the rape, I endured the preliminary trial. By mid-January of that same year, Charles stopped conversing with me.

During my first two semesters in college, I was seeing the counselor at school to talk about the rape and a counselor outside of school for the bulimia. I can remember sitting in class and writing down everything that had happened. I also remember engrossing myself in music, and at any opportunity, I engrossed myself in editing music videos.

It turned out that my love for one particular musician led to one of the most supportive friendships in my life. Julie tells the story of how we met during our first semester:

> *In those first few weeks at Point Park, I only knew Kristine as "that girl who sat across the room" during Journalistic Skills. She showed up to class and sat along the bank of computers on the right side of the room instead of at the table with most of the rest of us. She did her work and she left.*
>
> *Then, during a brief period in October, that girl simply wasn't there any longer.*
>
> *To be honest with you, I was having such a rough time trying to adjust to being on my own in a new city, surrounded by new people, that I didn't take much stock in that. My job was to go to class and get good grades. So, while I did notice that the girl who always sat on the right wasn't there, the teacher seemed to be okay with it, and I didn't really think about it again.*
>
> *I wish I could tell you that I remember when the girl came back, but I don't. I wish I could tell you that I*

*knew something was wrong immediately and that I
tried to help Kristine, but I didn't. I wish I could tell
you that it was obvious that she had been put through
something awful, but it wasn't. To put it simply: We
didn't know each other. We had one class together
and saw one another around. That was it.*

*Then one day in class, Kristine and I wound up sitting
next to one another. We did that brief talking thing
that people do, and after a few class sessions, we were
friendly, but we still weren't friends . . . until I
glanced at her computer during a break in class and
saw what Kristine was looking at.*

*To some, this may seem ridiculous, but I really think
that the roots of our friendship took hold because of
one person: Britney Spears. That day during the fall
of 2004 in Journalistic Skills class, Kristine was looking at something Britney-related. Upon realizing the
extent for Kristine's love of all things Britney, I admit-
ted my own. The rest, as they say, is history.*

*When Kristine and I started the spring semester of our
freshman year, we started hanging out. On the weekends, we would go to a hookah bar on the South Side,
and once it got nice out, we'd go for long walks
around downtown Pittsburgh at night.*

*A month into spring semester, I still had no idea what
Kristine had been through. Then one day, we were
faced with a mid-week, nothing-to-do, quiet night. I
followed Kristine to the café for a Diet Pepsi and then
to the smoker's lounge that was, for once, empty.*

*When we were casually talking about weekend plans,
Kristine told me that she was leaving Thursday night
because she had court Friday. I remember thinking to
myself that I didn't understand why Kristine would
have to go to court. She was a nice person who had a
good head on her shoulders. I wish I could tell you*

that I broached the topic lightly, but I don't remember how I asked, especially since Kristine's quick expla- nation was so blunt.

"I have to go to court because I was raped in Octo- ber."

I'm pretty certain I just sat there and didn't say any- thing. I know that I felt shocked and surprised and up- set that something like that could happen to someone who was such a good person. My surprise must have been obvious, because Kristine continued as if what she'd just told me was insignificant, shrugging her shoulders and then flicking the ash on her cigarette. "It's really no big deal."

I can remember feeling speechless and surprised by her complete lack of emotion over the whole thing. "I was raped in October. It's really no big deal."

It was almost as if Kristine were commenting on the weather. "Oh, look at the rain. By the way, I was raped in October. It's no big deal."

Kristine was incredibly nonchalant about the whole thing as she quickly told me the entire story. She did not cry. She did not get angry. She simply did not emote much of anything throughout the conversation, as if the incident were something she had seen on tel- evision and didn't have much of an opinion on what- soever.

Julie became my closest friend at Point Park. While she was con- fused about my lack of emotion in those early days after the rape, she accepted me and kept me busy. Over time, Julie came to understand my reaction:

I was there for the aftermath of Kristine's rape. I saw firsthand how it affected her. At first, I wasn't aware of how destructive it was, but after a few months, it was obvious that she really wasn't "over it" and that it really was a "big deal."

Sexual assault survivors often experience symptoms of Rape Trauma Syndrome, which occurs in two stages: the Acute (Initial) Phase is followed by the Reorganization Phase, which typically begins a few months after the assault and can last for years. Kristine was clearly still in this first phase when she told me about what had happened to her, which was demonstrated by her lack of outward emotion of the event.

The second phase, however, lasted much longer, and was obviously much more difficult for her to get through. During the first steps of Reorganization Phase, survivors tend to have very little regard for themselves. To make matters more complicated for her, Kristine was also dealing with an eating disorder, which gave her something to control when she felt she could not handle things any longer.

I remember spending days listening to Britney's greatest hits, or watching all her videos with Julie. Then I had the idea that Julie and I should film our own music videos. We created our first video together to a Britney song called, *"Do Somethin'."* We had so much fun creating it.

At the end of freshman year, I went back home to Johnstown for the summer. I began dating someone I will call Paul, who went to Penn State Altoona Campus (PSU), which is around 40 miles away from my family home in Johnstown. Paul was in the military and he was gone all summer, so we communicated via letters. At the end of the summer, I rode with Paul's parents and his little brother to his graduation ceremony from boot camp.

At the end of the summer, I was excited to return to Point Park for my sophomore year because I was going to room with Julie! I stayed on campus some weekends, and on other weekends, I went to see Paul at Penn State. We mostly partied when I was in Altoona, and I could never get Paul to come visit me in Pittsburgh. At some level, I knew that something wasn't right. One weekend, he had plans to come. I was so excited, and even had a pass filled out for him, but Paul cancelled at the last minute.

I found out from his roommate that there was a chance Paul was cheating on me. I can't remember if I ended the relationship first and beat Paul to the punch or not. But we broke up and I was both furious and distraught. Julie and I made a music video to the song *Kerosene* by Miranda Lambert, naming all the guys who had done us wrong. The list included my perpetrator and my crush from freshman year. At the end of the video, I ripped up a picture of Paul and me. The video symbolized a strong me, the person I wanted to be.

Underneath the strong exterior I portrayed in the video and in public, I was scared and broken. Thankfully, I was able to receive counseling through Pittsburgh Action Against Rape (PAAR) the semester I lived with Julie, but healing from any type of sexual assault is a painful process, even with the best of help.

I was stuck in a perception that I needed a relationship with a man to be valuable; at the same time, I was afraid of a real relationship and could only be intimate after a few drinks. I had put myself out on limb with Paul, hoping for a real relationship. When I learned that Paul might have been cheating, I was torn to pieces. I will never know if he really was cheating, but I did learn that Paul was "hanging out" with another girl when I wasn't around. They ended up dating after we broke up.

In light of this betrayal by yet another person I trusted, all I wanted was my mom. I wanted to go back to the comforts of being a child, when my mom used to care for me. Just a year earlier, immediately after the rape happened, I wanted nothing more than to move on from the incident. I felt that moving out of my hometown and never looking back was the answer. Now, I was longing so hard to go back. So, I made the decision to move home. I decided I would do a semester at the community college and figure out what I wanted to do next.

It was nice to be home, but I still spent a lot of time at PSU. I went there frequently on the weekends with Jenna, my girl-friend from high school. I think I was hoping to get back at Paul for what he did. I remember wanting to key his car with my high-heeled shoe after a party one night. I never got to try it, which is probably a good thing.

Because I was visiting PSU so frequently, I met a guy I'll call Greg. I then concluded that I wanted to attend school there. Looking back, it seems like I wanted to go there to chase after the new guy. So, I applied to PSU and got in. I was planning to have a double major in communications and psychology. My goal was to move to PSU in August 2006, moving into my junior year. During this time, Julie and I remained close friends. She continued her schooling at Point Park, and we got together as often as we could. She came to visit me in Johnstown close to the end of the spring semester. We took the opportunity to make two music videos, and had a blast.

Meanwhile, while I was switching schools, changing majors, partying, and chasing guys, my mom was worrying about me all the time. Her concern for me was all-consuming, even more dif-ficult than her own mother's death several years before.

Mom remembers when, roughly six months after my rape, the story of Natalie Holloway took center stage on the news. Na-talie had gone to Aruba on a senior high school trip. After leav-ing her friends at a bar and going off with two men, Natalie was never seen again. Seeing the similarities in the two instances, my mom sat glued to the television. She felt such a connection to Natalie's mom that she wrote a letter to her—and even received a reply.

Mom still was lacking someone in her daily life to talk with about her intense feelings. Dad didn't want to talk. My mom's sister-in-law, Sharon, was devastated by what had happened to me, but my mom still felt her sister-in-law couldn't connect with the pain of being a parent in this situation.

Mom was grateful for her counselor, and she talked to her about how my situation could have been worse—it could have been like Natalie Holloway's. The perpetrator might have killed me, or the stranger who called 911 for me might not have been looking outside that day. Even so, the horror of what *did* happen haunted my mom day and night.

In frequent conversations with the district attorney, my mom faced a dilemma. She understood that the perpetrator should pay for his crime, if only to prevent him from victimizing another woman. The DA wanted to press felony sexual assault charges and ensure the perpetrator was on the sexual predator list after serving his time.

Mom understood all this, but she also knew I didn't want to testify again. For her part, my mom wanted to protect me from reliving my whole trauma on the witness stand. Ultimately, the case was settled with a plea deal. This process, all-consuming for my mom, took two years. It wasn't until the legal case was behind us that my mom began to feel a bit of closure. To this day, my mom wouldn't say she is "over" what happened to me. My mom is healthy and happy, but she carries a scar always. Dad does, too.

During those two years, my mom thought about me constantly, but she only had so much energy. She was concerned about my emotional health, my education, the bulimia, and more. She might not have had the energy to realize how much I was partying and chasing guys.

As my perpetrator's legal issues ended, I was finishing my semester at the community college and enjoying my new boyfriend from PSU. I really liked Greg a lot. Everything seemed to be going great! I could move on with my new life in Altoona with my new boyfriend.

August rolled around and I transferred to the Olive Garden in Altoona to have a job while I went to school. I moved into an apartment with three other girls. Life was good. I had a few friends in Altoona, so I had a few people to hang out with besides my boyfriend.

In the fall of 2006, Greg and I were engaged. He even went to my dad to ask for my hand. At the time, the relationship was everything I could have hoped for. It had been two years since my assault, and I was starting to feel normal being intimate without having a few drinks beforehand. I was still having some difficulties with bulimia; it was easier to control but still there.

My parents liked Greg. He treated me well, and he focused on goals and objectives. We all believed that life was finally getting better.

The following spring, I made a couple of new friends in a French class I took as an elective. Both were in hospitality management, and that got me thinking. Greg was planning to transfer to main campus for his degree, but I didn't need to make the move for mine. When my new friends kept talking to me about hospitality management, I thought, "You know what? This could be the degree for me!"

I had worked in the restaurant industry for years, and the new major would allow me to transfer to main campus. Finding a job in the field would be easy because hotels and restaurants are everywhere! So, I changed my major.

The plan was to move up to main campus once classes wrapped up in May 2007, and I was going to move in with Greg. Little did I know that moving in was going to be the downfall of our relationship.

I said goodbye to my Altoona friends, telling them I couldn't wait to see them when they transferred to main campus. I found a summer job at the Nittany Lion Inn, a historic hotel located on campus. Greg got a job at a hardware store. We worked all summer.

Classes started up in the fall, and I was in a situation where the only person I knew in this new town was Greg. I didn't do much but spend time with Greg and work. I also never went to football games because I worked during most of them. I knew I could make a nice chunk of change if I worked during football games.

Greg and I moved in together in early summer, and it wasn't until September rolled around that our relationship began to change. One of my best friends, Dez, was turning 21 that month. Dez happened to have a boyfriend who lived at main campus.

I remember the day vividly. Greg was planning to go home to Johnstown for the night and he was to drop me off at Dez's boyfriend's so I could go with them for her 21st. Out of no-where, Greg began to yell at me. This hadn't been characteristic of our relationship, but it soon would be. At the time, I assumed Greg was upset that I was going out drinking with my girlfriend and he wasn't going to be there. I don't know if it was because he thought he couldn't trust me, but he had nothing to be scared about.

The next few months, my eating disorder slowly intensified as the stress between Greg and me increased. Sometimes, Greg would yell at me for trivial things. For example, one time when I went grocery shopping, Greg asked me to get something I had never bought before. He yelled at me for getting the wrong thing.

That fall, I also began to hold back on being intimate. At the time, I felt pressure because of the smell of fall. It may seem odd, but the smell was reminding me of the rape, and I felt uncomfortable being intimate. I began to immerse myself into my computer and mixing music videos instead of hanging out with Greg.

The tension between Greg and me got even more intense when I got involved in Rape, Abuse, and Incest National Network (RAINN) and joined their speaker's bureau. I don't remember how I first connected with RAINN, but I needed an outlet for the rape. Because I didn't want to testify, I needed another way to heal.

I got my first speaking opportunity at the University of Delaware. My Aunt Brenda and I went together because my mom was unavailable. Greg was adamantly against me speaking. He felt that I should stay silent. I remember calling him from the hotel before I went to the school to speak and begging him to wish me good luck. It was like pulling teeth.

If I remember properly, Greg mentioned that his mom had been raped and had chosen not to speak openly about it. Greg didn't want me to speak about my rape either, believing it would taint how others saw me. I, on the other hand, knew that my success in healing depended on me talking about what had happened to me. Greg's and my differences in responding to rape served as a divide between us on something that was very important to me.

In November 2007, I did some laundry before I left for my shift at the restaurant. While at work, I started to receive text messages from Greg informing me that I had shrunk his sweater in the laundry. I could sense him yelling through the text messages. I became upset at work. Greg must have realized that he shouldn't have said what he said, because he showed up at work with flowers and apologized. My boss let me leave early to be with him.

I thought that maybe I could fix the relationship, that the yelling was just a phase. But it wasn't. In the spring of 2008, I began to hang out with friends who had come up to main campus from Altoona. This allowed me to distance myself from Greg. I also learned of an opportunity for me to go to Italy over spring break with the Hospitality School, and I knew I wanted to do it. Greg was not a fan, but he let me go.

I must have known, in the back of my head, that the relationship was going downhill. I remember deliberately cutting my hair short because Greg liked it long. That past Christmas, Greg had gotten me a necklace, yet all I could talk about was the Spice Girl tickets my mom had gotten me. Mom had to remind me that Greg had gotten me the necklace.

Little indications provided clues that the relationship was eroding, but for some reason, I held on. I remember Julie mentioning that I should try to get an internship in Pittsburgh so that I could come and live with her for the summer. I thought it might be a good idea, so I began interviewing for a management internship with Red Lobster, the restaurant chain that I had worked for in high school. I got the internship. Greg did not want me to move to Pittsburgh, and I don't blame him.

Greg said something to the effect of, "If you go to Pittsburgh, does that mean we are breaking up?"

I said, "Yeah, I think we are."

And that was that. We were breaking up.

We agreed that we would live together until I moved to Pittsburgh because I had the rent paid until then. But after we broke up, I started to go out more, and sometimes a girlfriend would come over. One night, a girlfriend from work and I were sitting at the kitchen table. Greg came into the kitchen and began screaming at me that he would appreciate it if my friend left. He didn't like people that he didn't know in his home. My friend invited me to stay at her house because she was actually scared of what Greg might do. After being uncomfortable too often in similar situations with Greg, I decided not to wait until the lease was up to move out.

Once I moved to Pittsburgh, my life began taking some unexpected turns. I would meet my future husband during my internship, but I wouldn't be ready for the relationship yet.

CHAPTER 4

BRENDA, BRITTANY SPEARS, AND LADY GAGA

I SAW MY EX-FIANCÉ FOR THE LAST TIME in June 2008 at the notary office. Greg and I had to visit a notary to change the title of our trailer from my name to his. I knew this was most certainly a goodbye, not a-see-you-soon.

Three weeks were left before the start of my summer internship in Pittsburgh, where I would be living in an apartment with my good friend, Julie, again. A friend from school, whom I'll call Brenda, invited me to live with her family until it was time to move to the city. Brenda and I had gotten along well on a trip to Italy.

Those three weeks at Brenda's home were a whirlwind—mostly because I began to develop romantic feelings for my female friend. My two most recent relationships with men had been disasters. With Paul, my understanding of intimacy had been so distorted that I was able to be intimate only after a few drinks, and when that relationship ended in a betrayal, I was scared to be betrayed again

With Greg, I was so glad to get over the hurdle of being bolstered with a few drinks before being intimate; but then I had to deal with the eating disorder, depression, and other brokenness. Greg, although he professed to love me, couldn't handle my issues, including my need and desire to talk about my rape. What's more, he became verbally abusive. I walked away from that relationship because, in addition to feeling constrained and unable to be the person I wanted to be, I was afraid for my safety.

Perhaps in light of these experiences with men, it was natural that a relationship with a woman would seem nonthreatening and appealing. It made me feel safe. So, in June 2008, I began dating a girl.

Brenda and I had a lot of fun, partially because the relationship was a secret. We snuck around, hoping not to be caught together. We told a few friends from school, but that was all.

Toward the end of June, I moved to Pittsburgh for my 10-week internship at a Red Lobster. I was so excited to be back in the city. During the dark days with my fiancé, I had longed to be in Pittsburgh, mostly because of Julie. She was a great friend and sounding board throughout this ordeal.

For some reason, I felt uncomfortable telling Julie that I was dating a girl. I guess I was afraid she wouldn't accept me, although she gave no indication of that. I told a few other close friends, but I held back from telling Julie. Throughout the summer, I talked to Brenda quite a bit, and I felt bad because Julie thought that I was replacing her with my girlfriend. I reassured her I wasn't, but I'm sure that from Julie's perspective, my behavior didn't match my words.

My internship that summer was awesome. As an intern with Red Lobster, I was able to train in all the positions, from kitchen to dining room floor. I also learned manager tasks and responsibilities. The management team I worked with was great. They were all guys, but we got a long extremely well.

The manager nearest in age to me, JR, was new on the management team. I always enjoyed working with him. JR was laid back, easy going, and he made me feel comfortable. Like the other managers on the team, JR called me by my last name,

Honkus. I felt a true sense of comradery and trust with the all-male management team.

While I thought JR was attractive, I was involved with Brenda, and the relationship we shared was too new to be looking elsewhere for love. JR also had a romantic interest at the time, so the two of us became friends. JR invited Julie and me out one night after work to have a few beers and play pool. It was nice just to be able to hang out with a guy whom I considered a friend. I didn't have many male friends except Brandon, Pinkas, and Mark from high school.

That same summer, I decided to deliberately track my recovery process from rape through song. Christina Aguilera's song *Fighter* frequently stuck in my mind during this time, especially when I thought about the rape. The lyrics seemed to describe my own situation. Aguilera sings:

Well I thought I knew you, thinking that you were true.

I had certainly thought I knew my abuser when really I didn't. The lyrics continue:

After all of the stealing and cheating you probably think that
I hold resentment for you
But uh uh, oh no, you're wrong
'Cause if it wasn't for all that you tried to do, I wouldn't know
Just how capable I am to pull through
So I want to say thank you
Cause it

'Cause it makes me that much stronger

(Songwriters: Kenny Nolan, Robert Crese, © Sony/ATV Music Publishing LLC)

The rape was now nearly four years behind me, and I felt it *had* made me stronger. I wouldn't be who I was or where I was without having had the experience and everything that went with it. The song's refrain goes like this:

'Cause it makes me that much stronger
Makes me work a little bit harder
It makes me that much wiser
So thanks for making me a fighter
Made me learn a little bit faster
Made my skin a little bit thicker
Makes me that much smarter
So thanks…

Because the song described my perspective so well, I decided to get a tattoo saying *Fighter* across my right rib cage. I wanted the tattoo on the side opposite from my heart because my fight did not stem from love but from hurt and pain.

I also put two dates on the tattoo. I put the date of my birthday—because I was born premature and almost died after being born—as well as the date I was raped. God had made me a fighter from the beginning. So, I planned on using the song *Fighter* to create a music video.

I wanted to include some elements of the actual incident in my video, particularly when I was left on the side of the road. Filming in a cemetery would be ideal as well. I also thought about a boxing scene, and another scene in which I would have harsh words and dates fly at me as I hit them with a baseball bat.

I sat down with two friends and told them my ideas and they bounced back with theirs. Ideas began to come to life. My friends knew some people at a cemetery we could use, and they convinced me to change the concept with the bat; but I loved the plan and couldn't wait to put it together.

I was so excited on the day of the shoot. I had picked out two outfits to wear. We met early in the morning and shot all day. I remember being so nervous throughout the day. The shoot itself was a blast. I even got to break some glass with a brick.

Once the filming was completed, I was eager for my friend, Tom, to finish editing it. When he shared the result with me, I was completely floored. I could not believe the person in the video was *me*. It was *me* symbolizing how tough I truly felt. Some days I didn't feel that tough, of course, but the video reminded me of how strong I could be.

I remember showing the video to my mom, and her crying. She asked me if I actually got that tattoo and I said, "Yes."

Mom asked, "What do you think your future husband will think of that tattoo?"

I answered, "It doesn't matter what he thinks. I would hope he would accept me for who I am. If he can't do that, he is not meant to be my husband."

I showed the video to all my managers at work. In some cases, this involved sharing my story with some of them for the first time. They thought the video was awesome.

At the end of the summer, I was sad to leave my internship at Red Lobster. The managers offered to help me with anything I might need in the future. One top of that, the company offered me a full-time manager position with Red Lobster once I graduated.

When I moved back to PSU main campus in State College at the end of August 2008, I had my own apartment and a girlfriend. Brenda and I began to tell more people about our relationship, but we still did not tell our families. For both Brenda and me, this was our first relationship with a girl. I felt happy, safe and was comfortable in my relationship with Brenda, but deep down, I knew I would never tell my parents.

In retrospect, my mom says she saw a few signs to indicate that my relationship with Brenda was more intimate than a friendship. Mom, however, dismissed what she noticed, because

it didn't fit with her knowledge of me. I had always been interested in boys. It just didn't occur to her that I'd be in an intimate
relationship with a woman. After all, I had recently been engaged
to a man.

It wasn't until December 2008 that I finally told Julie about
Brenda. She was upset with me, not because of the relationship,
but because of the secret. I don't blame Julie, as I would have
been upset with me, too. I think I was scared I would disappoint
her. It turns out I disappointed Julie anyway by keeping something so important from her. Here's how Julie describes her reaction:

> *When Kristine finally told me that she and Brenda had
> decided to try a relationship, I was blindsided. Kris-
> tine had never shown any interest in girls before. As
> an independent Millennial, I consider myself open-
> minded. You should get to love whomever you choose,
> but when you go from liking boys pretty strongly one
> day to dating a girl a few months later, it's going to
> surprise your friends.*
>
> *All these years later, I can finally say that my hurt
> didn't stem from the fact that Kristine was in this rela-
> tionship, but from the fact that she purposely decided
> not to tell me. My hurt deepened when I returned to
> Pennsylvania and found out from a mutual friend that
> they had been dating for months, not the short period
> of time which Kristine had led me to believe. I still
> don't know why she felt she couldn't tell me. I'm not
> sure if Kristine thought I would be angry or disgusted,
> but she should have known that after everything she
> had been through, I would have supported her
> through this.*
>
> *All these years later, I can't imagine how hard it was
> for Kristine to hide this relationship. For someone
> who was so vocal about her sexual assault, it must*

*have been really difficult to be quiet about someone
she was in a relationship with.*

*Even though Kristine was taking this relationship se-
riously, I knew deep down that it wasn't a forever
thing. After all of the awful things that happened to
her—the assault, the eating disorder, and Greg, (the
guy who expected her to be barefoot in the kitchen
with three kids and no ambition)—I think Kristine
really was just trying to figure out who she was.*

My senior year in college went by extremely fast. One highlight
was that Britney Spears was finally out with new music. For me,
Britney Spears' music was there before and after the assault, but
not quite in the middle. Around the time of the assault, Britney
had gotten married. She went through a lot from 2004 to 2007
and took somewhat of a hiatus. Unfortunately, during the time I
most needed Britney's music was the time at which she stepped
away from it.

I was excited when Britney came out with her *Blackout*
album in 2007. When she came out with her *Circus* album in
2008, I dove completely back into her music. I was so happy
Britney came back on the music scene; I was in a new part of my
life, and the Queen was back!

During the spring of 2009, I saw Britney in concert three
times. I saw a concert in Pittsburgh with my mom, Julie, and
Brenda. Twice in May, I went to a show at the Mohegan Sun in
Connecticut with friends. I even shelled out for front row seats!
That was a surreal experience.

I could relate in a deep way to Britney because of her
breakdown. Before my rape, I didn't know that people had se-
crets or skeletons in the closet. Now I knew Britney was a human being, had feelings, and experienced depression and anxiety
just like anyone else.

The same year the *Circus* album was released, a new artist
named Lady Gaga emerged. I followed Lady Gaga and her music

closely because I related to it also. At the time, Gaga was all about being famous, but underneath there was a human being. Gaga had her persona and I knew I had mine.

Sometimes I felt like a variety of different people: the confident Kristine, the depressed Kristine, the tough Kristine, and the who-the-hell-am-I Kristine. When I listened to Lady Gaga's music, I felt I could embrace all my personas into one. Lady Gaga and her music had a healing effect on me. One sign is that during that same year, 2008, I finally conquered my eating disorder. I was starting to get more comfortable in my own skin.

I had put on some weight during the first eight months of my relationship with Brenda. So, I decided to start running, and when I did, some weight started to come off. Running would be another element that would come and go over the next few years until it became a regular practice.

As graduation approached, I began interviewing for other positions than the one at Red Lobster, just to have some options. I didn't want to rely completely on the one job offer, but nothing else came up. I was originally supposed to do my manager-in-training in Pittsburgh, but because Brenda still needed to finish her last few courses over the summer, I requested to do my training at the Red Lobster in State College. I was able to live with Brenda, have a full-time job, and enjoy State College one last summer.

As fall approached, Red Lobster was ready to transfer me to manage a restaurant. I was to choose between Dubois and Williamsport, both in Pennsylvania. I chose Williamsport, in North Central PA, nearly 200 miles from Pittsburgh, because it was bigger.

In September 2009, with Brenda freshly graduated, we moved to Williamsport. We found a place and were excited to start a new chapter together. On the other hand, my first week as a manager was depressing. I had a completely new level of responsibility, with over 80 employees to manage. Some were older and some younger than me, but I worried that not one of them was going to listen to me! Some days during that first week, I secretly cried in the bathroom. It was scary to have such a big job and scary to move to a new place, but at least I had Brenda.

As Christmas approached, I noticed a change in me. Without exactly deciding to, I started to distance myself from Brenda. Because my parents still didn't know about the relationship, I told Brenda I would prefer to spend Christmas with my parents without her.

Shortly after Christmas, my parents were renewing their vows in Vegas. Brenda and I went. We had fun, but no one there knew about our relationship. That's how I wanted it. Upon returning to Williamsport, while we were waiting for a ride to go home, Brenda looked at me and said, "I feel like I am starting to lose you." I assured Brenda she was mistaken, but deep down I knew she was right—and I knew why. I was starting to face the fact that I am attracted to men.

January 2010 was a pivotal month in my life because I was finally realizing I was hiding behind my relationship with a woman to shield my insecurities with men. Brenda and I had tickets to see Lady Gaga together that month in NYC at Radio City Music Hall, but we decided to take a break. I invited my Aunt Sharon to go with me to the concert, and we had a blast. I had gotten such good seats that we were a row behind Donald Trump! It was such a surreal experience, and Lady Gaga put on an amazing show.

Aunt Sharon knew I was dating a girl and that we had taken a break. At one point shortly after the concert, my aunt staged an intervention for me. She invited two lesbians who were good friends of hers to have an intervention. Honestly, it wasn't as dramatic as one would think. We just had dinner together while they asked me questions. They asked, "Who did I like in kindergarten?" "Who was my crush in high school?" As I answered the questions, it became increasingly clear that I was straight, which, of course, I already knew.

It was hard to return to Williamsport because Brenda was still living where we were renting. It was hard to let go because we had been in a relationship for a long time, and I didn't want to hurt Brenda. I ended up pretending that nothing had happened while I was away.

I continued to be distraught about the relationship. Then one day at work, I was so emotional, that a fellow manager, Kristin, pulled me into the office, shut the door, and said, "We are not leaving this office until you tell me what is going on."

I sat down and told Kristin everything about my relationship with Brenda. After a few days, I finally ended it with Brenda. It was hard and scary; not only because I didn't know what it would be like to date a guy again, but also because I knew it would break Brenda's heart. By then, of course, I knew that I didn't have a choice.

I haven't spoken with Brenda since we broke up, but I know she got married, and I can't begin to say how happy I am for her. I honestly wish Brenda and her family all the best.

In February 2010, I found myself, for the first time in six years, officially single. I had always told myself that I wanted the opportunity to live by myself and be on my own before I married. Now was the time. Brenda moved out, and I began to plan my summer.

I was looking forward to a trip Julie and I were planning to Las Vegas and Los Angeles for a wedding that summer. I also learned that Lady Gaga would be going on tour again in the fall and was coming to Pittsburgh! I ended up planning a Lady Gaga excursion and got to see the artist in Pittsburgh and again in Philadelphia!

I went all out for each of the two shows. I bedazzled my own leather jacket, rolled Diet Coke cans in my hair, and wore very big, black boots. Lady Gaga had an empowering speech during her show. Her core message was:

> *Tonight, I want you to forget all of your insecurities.*
> *I want you to reject anyone or anything that's ever*

*made you feel like you don't belong, or don't fit in, or
made you feel like you're not good enough, or thin
enough, or can't sing well enough, or dance well
enough, or write a song well enough, or like you'll
never win a Grammy, or you'll never sell out Madison
Square Garden. You just remember that you're a
superstar and you were born this way.*

Gaga made this statement at both shows, and even though I
have never won a Grammy, and most likely never will, it still
shook me to the core. It was so empowering for me. Being at the
concert allowed me to release all of my insecurities: blame and
guilt for the rape; not feeling accepted; and not loving my body.
As I listened to Gaga, I wasn't a victim, but a survivor, and I was
proud of it. I didn't care about my body, because God made me
beautiful, and everyone at the show that night knew it. We all
knew it about each other. After the Philadelphia show, I got a
tattoo on my wrist stating, "Born this way," to remind me of
that feeling of letting go of everything and just loving me.

Because I left Gaga's concerts feelings so amazing, I knew I
had to see her again. So, I planned a Lady Gaga vacation for
February 2011. I enlisted two great friends to go with me. We
drove to New York City, Washington, D.C., and Pittsburgh to
see her. Again, I went all out. The first show I wore a black body
suit with fishnets, a blonde wig, sunglasses, and a disco stick. For
the second show, I had to improvise because my costumes acci-
dentally got left in NYC. I wore a Lobster hat, a nude body suit,
and a leather jacket. For the Pittsburgh show, I wore a meat
dress. My friends and I were in the front row at that show, and
in the middle of a song, Lady Gaga looked at us and said, "Nice
meat dress." No one around me had on a meat dress, and the
moment is captured on YouTube.

Once my Lady Gaga trip ended, I was sad, but I knew more
healing through music was coming not only with Gaga, but with
Britney Spears, too!

I finally felt like things were really going the way I needed them to go. I hadn't had a relapse of bulimia since 2008. I still saw a counselor, as I had been all along. The counseling was helpful, but I was no longer depressed.

Julie does a good job of describing the change in me:

> *When Kristine and Brenda broke up and Kristine was on her own, I decided that I had been quiet for too long. I had been hurt by the fact that Kristine obviously had not wanted to tell me about this relationship. I had kept my thoughts to myself more often after I realized that. It was my job as a friend to support her. I felt that if I said anything, it would have come across as if I were being unsupportive.*

> *We had been friends for years, and in her past two relationships with men, I had witnessed Kristine losing parts of what had made her "Kristine" before. She had jumped from one long-term relationship to the next, and lost a part of herself in the process.*

> *I told Kristine that before she decided to date again, she needed to take some time for herself. She needed to take a year to figure out who Kristine was and what she wanted before she was ever going to be happy with anyone else. As I once heard a celebrity musician say, "You need to love yourself before you can love anyone else."*

> *Kristine took the time (not necessarily a year, but pretty close to it) to internalize and figure out who she was. For the first time, Kristine could go where she wanted simply because she wanted to. She could buy crazy Lady Gaga costumes and go on her own mini tour with Mother Monster if she wanted. She could drink wine with glitter in it if she wanted. She could move to Pittsburgh and continue with her career. She could drag me along to Philadelphia to meet Britney*

Spears and then stand in the front row at her concert and scream her lungs out.

For that year, Kristine may have been single, but she wasn't alone. She was surrounded by friends and family who supported her, and she, likewise, was there for anyone who needed her.

At the end of this "me" period, I discovered that the Kristine I now knew was someone whom I had never known before. She was stronger and smarter and much more independent than ever. She was fiercely loyal to her friends and family. She accepted everything bad that had happened, but instead of allowing it to control multiple parts of her life, Kristine let it simply become just a piece of her.

And when Kristine called and told me that she and JR had been hanging out and that she had feelings for him, I told her that quite honestly, I wasn't surprised. Sometimes we're at a crossroads and not ready for one thing, but when time and experience has come to pass and we come into our own, we can find the one person who seems to be our other half.

CHAPTER 5

TATTOOS, TRIPS TO PITTSBURGH, AND LEARNING TO LOVE

DURING THE TIME I WAS MANAGER in Williamsport, I sometimes called JR if something unusual came up in the restaurant and no other manager was available. Early in 2011, I started to call more often. One reason was that I had decided that I wanted to move back to the Pittsburgh region. I called to ask JR if he knew of any openings.

JR thought some openings would be coming up and promised to talk to his director on my behalf. Soon, JR's and my texts and phone calls became more frequent. I remember calling him one night to tell him that a drug dealer came into our restaurant searching for a server; I had never had that happen before. From there, our conversation led to random things that had happened in our restaurants. JR had a story about a woman who tried to attack her husband with a shoe. I knew I really enjoyed talking to him, and he was good friend, even though we were physically far apart.

That spring, I got a call about a manager's job opening in the Pittsburgh region. Could I move in the summer? I said, "Yes," and looked forward to the change. Meanwhile, I sometimes went to Pittsburgh for one reason or another. Each time, I contacted JR to see if we could get together. Once, four of us went to a Pittsburgh Penguins playoff game. We had a blast, and I drove home to Williamsport afterwards.

In May, a few months before I was scheduled to move, I decided to have a more elaborate tattoo placed on my right side. I connected with an artist in Pittsburgh who had been recommended to me. I wanted to add a scroll around my *Fighter* tattoo. This tattoo would symbolize my healing. A rose over the scroll would symbolize me. That rose would droop and drip onto the word, *Fighter*, representing the pain I had experienced. This would show how the rape coats my existence, even as I continue to heal. As the final element to the tattoo, I planned side-by-side roses to symbolize my parents. These roses would show that the rape not only affected me, but my family as well.

This tattoo, obviously, would take a number of sessions. For the first session, I took two days off around the appointment so I could plan a road trip. I enlisted my cousin and a girlfriend to come to Pittsburgh with me. I called JR to ask if we could crash at his place for a night. Once JR said, "Yes," the three of us drove to Pittsburgh and went out with JR. The next day, I got my tattoo started.

I made four trips to Pittsburgh to get work on done on my tattoo before I actually moved to Pittsburgh. One time, JR and I met for drinks and an appetizer. We were in a funny phase at that point. I knew I had feelings for JR, and it seemed like he had feelings for me, but I wasn't sure. He gave me a quick kiss after those drinks and appetizers, but it was awkward. We laugh about it now, and talk about how horrible and awkward that kiss was.

I didn't get to see JR every time I came to Pittsburgh, but sometimes it worked out. In between visits, we called and texted frequently. I remember one day when my mom and I came down to look at apartments for my upcoming move. I took my mom to the tattoo parlor where I had been getting work done, and then we went out to dinner. I invited JR to join us for dinner, but he said he would only come for a drink afterwards. I understood; we weren't really dating, so it might be weird to "meet the parent."

At the end of July 2011, it was finally time to move to my new apartment in the Pittsburgh suburb of Monroeville. My parents and a friend came to help me unload. Because he got stuck in traffic, JR showed up just in time to get the last piece, a couch, into the apartment. I ended up hanging out with JR that night and staying at his house. He drove me to get my rental car in the morning.

JR waited for me to get everything at the rental car place, just in case something didn't work out. I remember walking outside after I got the car keys, only to hear Janet Jackson's *Escapade* blaring and see JR dancing in the car. All I could do was laugh. I came over to the window and scared the crap out of JR. I will always remember that image.

I had a full week off to move, and I took that time to go camping with Kristen, whom I had worked with in Williamsport, and then on to a Britney excursion with Julie. We got to meet Britney Spears, which fulfilled a childhood dream of mine. When I returned to settle into my new home in the Pittsburgh area, JR was one of the few friends I had there. At this point, JR and I were "talking." I'm not even sure what "talking" means. It was as if we were friends but moving into a romantic relationship and not ready to say so aloud.

The months of August and September passed in a blur. At some point in the early weeks, romantic feelings started to come out, and JR and I began to acknowledge those feelings. We agreed we didn't want anything serious. JR had just gotten out of a serious relationship, and I was okay with moving slowly. Neither of us had any idea that there was a bigger plan for us.

I remember hanging out at JR's community pool one day when we both had off work. We sat around the pool listening to 80s and 90s music, taking turns guessing the artist and title of the song. We talked about our lives and our childhoods. That night, we went out to dinner with some of JR's friends, Bethany and

Jason, whom I was meeting for the first time. I remember worrying that they wouldn't like me, but it all worked out. Bethany and I are still close many years later.

I remember another date day that summer, when JR came over to my apartment. I am not much of a cook, but I cooked enchiladas for lunch and chicken parmesan for dinner. We also went to the movies for the first time and saw *Horrible Bosses*.

Another day, JR went to visit his parents, told them about me, and acknowledged that he really liked me. His biggest concern was that I dressed up in costume to go to concerts. If I remember correctly, no one in the family was too concerned. Plus, they thought that by the time I was 30 or so, the dressing up would stop. (Just an FYI, it hasn't.)

When September rolled around, I got my first sign that JR might be the man I should marry—because an incident that might have totally embarrassed me with any other person didn't embarrass me at all with JR. Several of my friends and I were heading to Vegas for a week, and JR was going to drive us to the airport so we didn't have to pay to park.

It was my time of the month, so I asked JR if I could use his bathroom, and I did. While in Vegas, I got a call from JR, asking me if I had left anything on the back of the toilet. I immediately realized that I had left my wrapped feminine product on the toilet rather than place it in the trash. I had been in a hurry. JR noticed and took care of the problem before anyone else went into his bathroom. While this might have been very embarrassing, it just seemed okay with JR.

The bathroom story is just one example of how comfortable I felt with JR. He knew about my past before we began to date, so that was no barrier. JR had been one of the managers at Red Lobster who saw my *Fighter* video during my time as an intern. Here's what JR says about his initial reaction to my story:

> *Before I met you, my feelings on rape culture were much like those of most other members of society. I assumed that rape doesn't happen that often, but*

when it does happen, it is a brutal crime. I hadn't known anyone who had been raped before I met you. While I thought rape was terrible, I didn't expect it to happen to me or anyone I knew.

After I met you and I heard your story, my feelings changed. I realized then that there had been times in college when incidents involving sexual assault could have been happening right in front of me, maybe at a bar or at a house party. Back then, it hadn't occurred to me to think, "This is a drunken girl who needs someone to make sure she is safe." I usually thought, "It's good that guy is taking that girl home so she doesn't get arrested for being drunk."

I don't know for sure if I was witnessing sexual predators on the prowl, but ever since we have been together, those concerns enter my mind consistently. Could I have stopped this from happening to someone else?

I feel like I should say that I felt bad or sorry for you when I learned about your past. But that would be a lie. Instead, I felt encouraged by you. You told me by showing me your own personal artistic way for dealing with the rape, and then just owning it, and telling me what had happened. I don't mean you owned it in a way where you were taking responsibility. Rather you owned it by pointing out, "This happened to me and look at me; I'm still right here; it hasn't stopped me and it won't."

In that moment, I felt you had complete control over yourself and found strength in yourself, as well as determination to tell your story. I'd be lying if I didn't say that it was a little intimidating to see how confident you were in something that I imagined anyone being completely timid to talk about.

The subject of my rape came up occasionally in conversations when JR and I were friends—and more when we began to date. JR was open, accepting, and willing to take me as I was. I never got the sense that JR wanted to change me or rein me in. My advocacy for rape victims and for culture change surrounding rape was fine with him. Because of JR's acceptance of my past and his willingness for me to choose my own path to healing, intimacy came easily.

It wasn't long after I came back from Vegas that I got a second sign that JR might be my one-and-only. One morning when I was staying at JR's house, he asked me what I wanted from Sheetz for breakfast, and I said I didn't know. JR told me that if I didn't tell him what I wanted, he was going to get the whole menu. He literally came back with the whole menu. I never had anyone do that for me. I was floored, and my heart was full of joy.

I also remember the first time I met JR's mom, Melinda. She came to Pittsburgh for a visit, and I happened to be available to meet her before JR got home from work. Decorating JR's house for Halloween and building a bonfire, Melinda and I immediately bonded. That night was the first of many great times together. I'm grateful to have Melinda and her husband, Jim, as my in-laws.

My memories of the fall of 2011 are filled with great times with JR. When October 10th, the anniversary of the rape, came around that year, for the first time I didn't cry about what had happened to me. I woke up that day with JR next to me. I didn't even think about the rape until my friend called me to tell me that my perpetrator was in jail for another crime. When I got off the phone, I turned to JR and said, "Do you know what today is?" I told him about the anniversary. I also said, "This is the first time in seven years that I haven't woken up crying or feeling bad for myself or blaming myself." I give a lot of credit to JR because he was such a positive influence in my life.

For example, it wasn't until I met JR that I was able to re-connect with God. I was raised a Catholic, and went to a Catholic school from kindergarten to 12th grade. Religion had been a big part of my life, but once at college, I didn't have anyone pushing me to go to church. Like many college students, I went on Christmas, Easter, and any other time I was home to visit my family.

I can't say that I was really angry with God about the rape; that isn't the reason I turned away from him or didn't go to church. I still prayed. I didn't pray for my healing, but I prayed for other things, such as family, friends, and finding true love.

JR and I were engaged on February 25, 2012, at a Pittsburgh Penguins hockey game. Along with other things, we began discussing what kind of church we would get married in. We originally began looking at Catholic churches, and, at the same time, JR took me to a Presbyterian church he attended every now and again. This church began to grow on me more and more.

As time went on, I told JR that I wanted to become Presbyterian, and I wanted us and our future children all to go to one church. This decision came easily for me because JR did not push me; he was allowing me to make my own decision. This was very different from when I was previously engaged because I had felt like I was being forced to in a sense "lose my religion." The religion I had grown up with and knew was being forced away from me. With JR, there was no pressure, and I was free to make up my own mind.

I officially became Presbyterian sometime in 2012, and we were married at a Presbyterian church in Pittsburgh by the pastor from the church JR and I were attending. Once we were married, moved into our house, and needing a new church, we found out the pastor who had married us got a new job at a church 15 minutes from our new home. If that wasn't a sign from God, I don't what is. We immediately joined and got involved in many aspects of our church. By doing this and now having such amazing church family has truly helped my healing.

The support we receive from the church is tremendous and really puts God's work into perspective.

I was finally able to realize that while Lady Gaga did help me learn to love myself, God played a much bigger role. JR always says that God gives the toughest battles to his strongest soldiers, and I am a firm believer in that. I also believe that God never intends for bad things to happen. God loves us and grieves with us when bad things happen to us. He is there with us during the darkest times of our lives, providing us with a lantern to guide us to hopefully make the right decisions in the process.

Between JR's love and my renewed relationship with God, I was feeling more and more empowered. Fresh ideas about my continued healing and advocacy were starting to flow. Ultimately, I came to see that God had been guiding me in this healing process and, with his love, I could fulfill my true calling of being a wife, mother, and an advocate.

I don't remember how I got the idea to write letters to all of my family and friends to inquire about how my rape had affected them. I just knew I wanted to know how my loved ones felt and how my rape had affected them. I had come to realize that a person's rape affects everyone who loves her or him. Initially, I had been so caught up in my own pain and struggle to heal, that I hadn't understood that those who supported me were hurting too. Little did I know how much I would learn from this project.

I began writing letters to individuals, including my aunts, uncles, cousins, friends, and even my mom and dad. Because there is so much emotion around my rape, it wasn't always easy for me to write and give these letters. I was able to give the letters to some people right away, while it took me over a year to give my letter to my dad.

I was so nervous to give my dad the letter, and surprised when he was happy to receive it. Dad was excited that someone actually asked him to share his feelings—because even 10 years after my rape, no one had ever asked.

People have responded differently to my asking about their feelings. While it took me a year to give my letter to my dad, he was able to respond within a few weeks. Some of the people I've asked about their feelings have not yet been able to respond.

While I was writing, receiving, and processing the information surrounding the letters, JR and I were planning our wedding. While my letter-writing project brought up many emotions, it did not dampen my joy in JR and in our future together. Our wedding day on March 23, 2013, was absolutely amazing and beautiful. It was wonderful to be surrounded by friends and family that loved us so much. The assault was the last thing on my mind that day.

In October 2013, when the anniversary date of the incident rolled around yet again, I felt a sense of empowerment more than any other emotion. Perhaps the healing that came with JR's unconditional love, or the letters I received from others, sparked my deeper and deeper desire to advocate for other victims of rape and sexual assault.

Early in 2014, I became involved in a campaign called Red My Lips. This campaign challenges women and men to wear red lipstick or show support for survivors in other ways for the entire month of April, which was challenging for me, because I don't typically wear bright lipstick. I wore red lipstick occasionally in April to show my support. I also started to share current events on my Facebook page and follow the news when it came to sexual assault. My role as an advocate was growing.

In the fall of 2014, I had the opportunity to speak at Youngstown State University. This was the first time JR would hear me speak. He sat in the back of the crowd, and when I got to the part of my presentation about him, I lost it. I was just so grateful to have JR in my life.

I got a question that night about how I had learned to trust again. I don't know if I gave the answer that I wanted but I can say for certain, it took time. I hope that when I speak, I help just one person to realize he or she can pull through and learn to trust again. Rape survivors never fully recover, but they can still live a full life.

In the fall of 2014, I found out I was pregnant. The day that JR and I told our parents was the 10-year anniversary of my rape. How crazy is that? Something that happened that was horrible 10 years earlier was now turning into a date I will forever treasure because of my baby. News of my baby turned that day into a positive, and as I write this, I can feel the tears welling up in my eyes because that baby was a blessing; another blessing in my life that would allow me to heal even further.

MY RAPE AFFECTED EVERYONE WHO LOVED ME

NO MATTER HOW STRONG I BECOME, or how surrounded by love I am, the rape experience will always be a part of me. At least on one level, I will never completely heal. On another level, the experience holds little power to define me. In fact, each time I tell my story to help others, I get stronger.

Around the 10-year anniversary of the rape, I began to reflect upon the incident from a different perspective. I began to realize that my rape had deeply affected those who loved me and surrounded me at the time. Because of the intensity of my trauma, I had been too self-focused to see this. Now I began to see that the violence of rape ripples out from the victim to that person's family and friends. I began to realize that in our culture, we don't acknowledge or talk about this ripple effect—and we should.

For example, it was years before I learned how devastated and isolated my mom felt in her grief over what had happened to me. If I had broken a leg or gotten cancer, people would have sent cards, baked casseroles, and expressed their concern. Because I was broken by rape, my parents suffered in silence and isolation. Mom struggled through work every day believing she couldn't tell others what had happened to me. My father turned his anger against God and is only now beginning to regain his faith.

As you know, it was around the 10-year milestone that I asked those who loved me at the time of incident—as well as those who came to love me afterwards—to write about their experience of my rape. In this chapter, I share their experiences, mostly in their own words.

My parents, of course, were the ones most affected by my trauma. Their stories are detailed in other chapters. My friend Julie's story is as well. Here are the stories of others who shared their experience with me at year 10.

PINKAS—CHILDHOOD FRIEND

My relationship with Pinkas dates from our kindergarten classroom. Pinkas was one of my closest friends at the time of the incident. We were as much like brother and sister as we were friends.

Pinkas saw the danger signs in my association with the guys from the convenience store from the start. In fact, he and Mark were the ones who insisted on going with me to the first party in the cemetery. Pinkas knew the convenience store guys were bad news, and he was concerned about protecting me. Since he was headed to boot camp as I was headed to college, Pinkas asked Mark to step up and protect me from these guys and my own bad decisions.

Pinkas was in boot camp at the time of the incident, and allowed only on Sundays to read letters he had received that week. I sent Pinkas a letter, explaining that something happened but that I was okay. I didn't want to tell him exactly what had happened because I knew he had to concentrate on his training.

When Pinkas graduated from boot camp shortly before Thanksgiving, he learned about the rape in a phone conversation with a friend. Here is how Pinkas describes it:

My heart completely dropped. My oldest friend, the one I consider a sister, had this terrible thing happen. Not only was I not there to stop it, but I wasn't there to help her recover. I felt terrible. Even in my worry, I had never imagined something so horrible or wrong had happened to Kristine. I wanted to hurt the guys that did this to her, but knew I had to wait to talk to her.

My heart grew with anger, not only toward the guy who wronged Kristine—I was upset with her too. In my mind, she allowed herself to get into that situation. I was also angry with myself for not attempting to stop the friendship she was making with those guys when I felt something was off. I felt I should have done more and maybe none of this would have happened.

While Pinkas learned about my rape in November, we didn't get a chance to see each other face-to-face until February. During those in-between months, Pinkas' anger with me remained steady. He describes how his emotions changed when we talked:

On one of my days at home on leave, Kristine and I went to Eat'n Park for breakfast. At this point, I was still filled with anger. I didn't know how I was going to express what I was feeling without hurting or upsetting Kristine.

Kristine started to tell me about the events that led up to that dreadful night, particularly about the night Erin and her dad had to take care of her and bathe her. Kristine explained how everything began to spiral for her, up to the point that she was found on the side of the road. Suddenly, I was no longer angry, upset, or mad at Kristine.

As she told me her story, Kristine's eyes started to water, and it seemed as if every other sentence she was

*saying, "I'm sorry, Pinkas." My anger instantly dis-
appeared, and I felt so helpless and ashamed of myself
for being mad toward Kristine. Most of all, I felt sor-
row that someone I consider more like a sister than a
friend had this terrible event happen to her. I lost my
appetite. I felt like I was going to throw up, and I was
shaking as I reached across the table and grabbed her
hand. I told Kristine not to be sorry, that it wasn't her
fault. I meant every word. To this day, that was the
worst meal of my life.*

*Throughout my career as a master at arms, I have had
to deal with rapes and sexual assaults. Because of
Kristine's incident, I honestly feel that I am more
aware and seem to get more sympathetic toward the
victims I encounter in my job. I see the aftermath and
destruction rape causes, not only in the victim, but also in those who render aid and support to the victim.*

*Everybody has a story, and I hope that through Kris-
tine's efforts, rape will gain more attention and people will come out, speak out, and support one another.*

COURTNEY—FRESHMAN YEAR COLLEGE ROOMMATE

Courtney and I met in September 2004 and bonded over our
love for Britney Spears, pop music, and our excitement for the
future. We hung out together and had a lot of fun. Things
changed when I called her from my parents' home in October.

Like Pinkas, Courtney felt anger at my perpetrator and guilt
that she had been unable to protect me. Unlike Pinkas, Courtney
got caught in my downward spiral as I tried to process the rape.
She describes it this way:

*At the end of October, Kristine and I both went home
for the weekend. I hugged her goodbye and told her I
would see her Sunday night, when we would catch up
and giggle about everything that had happened over
the weekend over pizza. When I came back to Point*

Park on Sunday night, she wasn't back yet, which was odd. It wasn't until my phone rang that night and I answered that everything changed.

Kristine sounded scared, and I asked her if she was okay. No. No. She wasn't okay. She went on to tell me that she was in the hospital because she had been raped and wouldn't be back to school for a while. Raped: It is a word that I had never had to wrap my mind around before. At 20 years old, you still don't know how to react to your new best friend being raped. I asked Kristine what had happened. She had been at a party, drinking alcohol and a guy took her, raped her in a cemetery, and left her for dead on the side of the road, like roadkill.

How can someone be so inhumane? What kind of monster does this to a beautiful, young girl? The emotions I felt were all over the charts. I felt that I should have been there to save her. When you live with someone, you kind of feel responsible for them, and something bad happened to her and I wasn't there to stop him or help her.

I felt angry. Angry because I wanted to hurt this guy who did this to her. I was mad at Kristine's friends and everyone at the party that had let him take her away.

I remember hanging up the phone with Kristine and just sitting on her bed sobbing. You hear about sexual assault and rapes every day on the news, but not until there is a face or a name of someone you know associated with rape that it hits you differently from there on out.

I remember when Kristine came back to school. At first, I didn't know how to react or how to treat her. How do you treat a rape victim? Do you walk on eggshells? Act as if it didn't happen? Talk about it open-

ly? Wait for her to bring it up? All of these questions, with no answers.

When Kristine returned to school, things changed. We both became self-destructive to an extent. Drinking, smoking, excessive workouts, not showering, sleeping more than we were awake, not going to class consistently, and looking for attention in all the wrong places. In November, I got sick and was in and out of the hospital until I had surgery in February. We were not healthy, and it showed.

Kristine began making videos to popular pop artist songs, and I believe that was an outlet for her. It was a way to distract herself from what had happened, a way to get emotions out, and to try to find a way to be herself again. We made it to the end of the semester, and after a long, emotional, fun year she and I remained best friends; however, we roomed with different people the following year.

Kristine and I remained close. We would talk about her attacker, and I remember the details of the trial. All I wanted was to go and berate him for what he had done to her. I am very protective of my friends, and the fact that he raped her and was just fine while she was suffering never sat well with me.

Once Kristine graduated from school, her life began to fall into place. She worked her way up in Red Lobster; she met JR, married him; and she is now a glowing mom. It amazes me how far she has come. Watching her grow and mature from a 19-year-old girl who was left for dead, into a beautiful, successful wife and mom is one of the best feelings in the world. It goes to show you how God works in mysterious ways. Kristine was handed a struggle, and she overcame and is victorious.

Since the incident, my feelings on sexual assault, victims, and rape have changed drastically. Before it happened to someone I was close to, I never thought about these things. Now, when I see sexual assault on the news, hear it from a friend, or even hear Kristine talk about it, it brings all those feelings and emotions back. I have agreed to wear red lipstick in April for Red My Lips [campaign to raise awareness about sexual violence], but why limit it to just April? It's good to always take a stand for what you believe in and spread the word.

CHRIS—CHILDHOOD FRIEND

On the weekend of the incident, not wanting my parents to know I was home to see my crush, I asked Chris if I could spend the weekend at his apartment. Another childhood friend, Mark, was with Chris when I insisted upon leaving with my perpetrator. When I didn't come back to the apartment that night, Chris and Mark feared the worst. They drove around looking for me without success. Chris describes it as follows:

The next morning, a paramedic transporting Kristine to the hospital answered her phone when we called. We found out that she had been victimized and then left by the side of the road. I felt a bit like I'd failed her, as it was my place she was supposed to be staying at that weekend. I could have been more of a voice of reason, especially given that we had some concerns about these guys.

When I saw Kristine at the hospital, it was just all about relief. I was sorry to see her in the shaken-up, disoriented state she was in, but I was glad Kristine was still with us and knew she would get through it, and that we could try to help her do so.

Prior to Kristine's experience, rape had been a serious issue, but one from which I was somehow de-

*tached. I was unaware that rape could touch my life
and my friends. Rape suddenly became real to me. We
like to shield ourselves from harsh realities sometimes, I suppose.*

*In my role as a mandated reporter in the mental
health field, it's my duty to report any suspected
abuse/neglect. Having witnessed firsthand what violence can do to someone definitely contributes to my
desire to safeguard others from experiencing it. I lost
some naiveté through Kristine's experience; to this
day, I nag at my girlfriend when she chooses to walk
through Pittsburgh neighborhoods alone without pep-
per spray.*

*I haven't felt guilt, per se, because Kristine was al-
ways a strong-willed individual. If she wanted to walk
into a tornado, she was going to do it, with or without
anyone's consent. I wish I had had the words to talk
her out of going out that night, but nobody would
have. I know the path Kristine ultimately chose after
the rape has led her to some pretty great outcomes,
and I was proud to see her find true love and start a
family. Hers is a story of strength triumphing over ad-
versity.*

BRANDON—CHILDHOOD FRIEND

Brandon, like many of my friends, felt shocked and helpless in
the face of my trauma. Like the others, he felt frustrated and betrayed at the outcome of the legal case against the perpetrator.
Here are Brandon's words about his experience:

*Finding out what happened to Kristine was pretty
scary and shocking. It was an eye-opening experience.
At the trial, I saw the perpetrator's face for the first
time, and it upset me. I drove by his house a couple
times to look for his car. One time I saw him at a bar,
and my friends had to pull me out of the place. I got*

pretty close to him and a friend side-tackled me to get me away.

I thought the verdict was messed up. The perpetrator was able to just get off and go back out in the world. I just felt so sad. I felt bad for Kristine. I was not trying to figure out the right words to say to her, but also not saying the normal things I say to her. It was hard because she was such a big part of my life; she's awesome. When something like this happens to someone close by, there's nothing any one can do.

Kristine's direction changed after the incident. I believe there are different ways people can react to rape, positive or negative. Kristine tried to figure out herself again, including everything she was going through, and she picked a path and followed it. I don't know how she feels every day, but I know the incident changed her to be stronger and more alert.

Kristine took a positive approach, not only for herself, but also for others. She loved making videos, and dance was a passion. She made a video about being a survivor, and went to her old dance studio to perform. Putting herself out there was her way of dealing with it. I think she did it positively and I believe it altered her life.

JENNA—CHILDHOOD FRIEND

Jenna was one of the friends who had been with me before the incident and who attended the trial. Like many of my friends, she felt that my perpetrator got off easily. Jenna is also one of the friends I told about my relationship with my girlfriend. None of my friends judged that relationship, but many felt my decision to be with a girl was more connected to my trauma than my true sexual orientation. Here's how Jenna tells her story:

You think, "Oh my gosh, this really happened to my friend." It was one of those times where you are grief-

stricken because this is something that happened to your friend, and there is nothing you can do. I don't recall the next time I saw Kristine, but I know things were different. Something completely changed in her life. It was a tragic moment.

I know we weren't responsible for the incident because there is no way we could have known it was going to happen. But our friend, Pinkas, knew something was up with those guys she was hanging out with. I never personally met the perpetrator, but I wonder what I might have done differently if I had understood the danger. Would I have told Kristine to call her mom and dad to let them know she was home? Would I have made her stay at my place that night? Would I have contacted her more? Rather than blaming us, I ask myself what we could have done differently.

We had to go to the preliminary hearing with her, and we had to go and tell the day's events. It was different; she had had a huge traumatic thing happen to her. She didn't show it at first—she was so young—but you could tell she was a different person. Kristine went from being a girl who had all these fun times, to "Oh my gosh, this happened."

The hearing didn't go in her favor at first. It felt like it was drawn out much longer than it should have been. I felt the perpetrator didn't show any remorse or anything toward Kristine, such as sympathy. The hearing took forever. I felt so bad for her, especially having to relive the incident after she had gone through it.

The perpetrator definitely didn't get enough justice. He got probation rather than a jail sentence. I felt frustrated, upset, and dissatisfied. It made me feel I couldn't do anything for Kristine except be there for her and listen. The trial definitely didn't have the outcome it should have.

You see rape dramatized on TV, and it's one of those things that you never think will happen to anyone you know. Especially someone you have known for four or five years at the time. It was crazy. Seeing a friend go through something like this definitely makes you think twice about your priorities and about letting people know what is going on.

I remember having that conversation with Kristine about her girlfriend. She was nervous to tell anyone about the relationship. I'll support Kristine no matter what she does, but after the rape, it was hard for her to trust a man, to have a masculine person in a relationship.

Kristine had been engaged previously. She's a very strong person, but he tore her down, he wasn't supportive, and he wasn't the person that she should ever end up being with. It wasn't that his masculinity threatened her, but the relationship put her in a place that might have reminded her of the rape, because her fiancé was someone who was not emotionally there for her. So she needed someone who was nurturing and there for her. I think that's why she went to that place and had different views. I can totally understand why she went that way.

ERIN—CHILDHOOD FRIEND

If anyone could have seen the disaster coming, it was Erin. She and her dad were the ones who cleaned me up from a drunken stupor when I first started to hang out with the guys from the convenience store. Erin was at Duquesne University when the rape occurred. Here is how she describes her feelings upon hearing my story:

I certainly remember when Kristine called me to tell me what had happened to her. I actually knew all about what had happened from friends, but I had waited to hear about it from Kristine.

When I first heard, I did not want to call Kristine to talk because the first emotion I felt was anger. I was so mad that she had gone out with those guys again, and even angrier with them. I couldn't comprehend my anger, so I just distanced myself from Kristine.

I know that my response to her phone call to me was probably not at all what she had wanted. I still feel a lot of regret about that. I should have been there for Kristine, because the rape was not her fault. At the time, I think I blamed her for all of it because I needed a scapegoat, even though I knew those guys were the real culprits. I kept distancing myself and expressing my true emotions of sadness and absolute anger toward those guys to friends rather than to Kristine.

I kept letting Kristine go down this destructive path at Point Park even though I wanted to stop her. I knew she had to deal with all of this in her own way. I wanted to take it all away from Kristine, but I couldn't. I joined in on the parties and the smoking. I thought that this was helping her. I know now that I should have done things differently. However, I also know that Kristine is Miss Independent. She would have continued to deal with things the best way she had seen fit.

I think I went down a bad path with Kristine as well. I was letting us both deal with things destructively because I thought that at some point we would snap out of it. I hated being at Duquesne at first, because I missed home. I wanted everything to go back to the way it was that summer before we left for college. I just thought everything changed for the worst, and I felt so empty inside. I made all of Kristine's feelings second to mine. Again, I still feel guilty about all of that. I did not know how to be there for Kristine, so I just let us keep living how we miserably wanted to live.

I think things just somehow moved forward, and any emotions we truly felt were never really discussed. I felt like we would never have the same kind of inno-cent friendship we used to, and I did not know what that would mean for us down the road.

AUNT BRENDA—MY MOTHER'S SISTER

I've been fortunate to remain connected with many of the peo-ple who were close to me at the time of the incident. Many of them have observed that the experience of rape, from a devastat-ing beginning, has ultimately made me a stronger person. I agree. Although I would not wish for anyone to experience rape, I know that my choice to reclaim my own way in the world has made me the person I am today. The journey itself has been hor-rible, but I am a strong person now, with a mission to help oth-ers. My Aunt Brenda talks about this in her story:

I remember the day when my husband, Kevin, listen-ing to his scanner, heard about the police finding a girl on the side of the road in Richland Township. I was working at the time. When I got home, Kevin told me that my brother-in-law had called for me. He hadn't said what he wanted or that I needed to call back.

I don't remember when I found out that it was my niece, Kristine, who had been left on the side of the road and had been a victim of sexual violence. I wished they had called me at work. I would have left my job to go to the hospital to be there for my family.

I remember how upset my sister, Tina, was about the legal proceedings. She would call and talk to me about how things were going and how hard it was for everyone to go through. In 1996, the federal govern-

ment had passed a law that made Kristine's perpetrator's crime a felony.

The perpetrator was not convicted of a felony in this case; he pleaded guilty and got probation. For such a serious crime, I never understood why that was all he had to do. I feel that sometimes our criminal justice system does not stand up for victims of sexual violence.

A few years later, my sister called and asked me to go with my niece to Delaware. Tina was unavailable and could not go with Kristine. My niece wanted to go to a college and talk about being a victim of sexual violence. I wanted to be there for her, so I said I would go. This was the first time she was going speak publicly since the rape had happened.

I was glad Kristine was going to talk about what had happened. I know it was very hard for her to stand in front of people and relive the incident again. Sitting there listening while Kristine talked to the group and took questions afterwards, I was proud of her for speaking out about sexual violence. I hadn't realized that Kristine had not remembered much of what had happened because of the alcohol. I felt her going to talk to other young people made them aware of what can happen and helped prevent them from being a victim. Too many victims are afraid to speak out.

I wasn't sure what the future would bring for Kristine. I know sometimes that it is hard to move on after a sexual violence attack and to trust someone again. I was glad when Kristine became engaged and then married to JR.

Kristine continues to speak out for victims. She has joined the campaign of Red My Lips and is planning events in support of victims. Her husband supports her and has given her extra confidence to speak out. I

*have prayed that God would bless her with a happy
life and am so glad she and her husband joined a
church where they live this past year. I really feel that
with the love and support from their families, victims
can survive the dark times after a sexual violence attack. In time, they can be happy and healthy and live a
full life.*

ERIN—PART 2

This excerpt from Erin's letter continues the theme of healing
and hope for the future:

*I could not believe that nothing ever came of your
case, and that those guys got away with so much.
However, I do believe that YOU are so much stronger
because of this. You overcame so much, and I am
proud to say I know the stronger, wiser, more beautiful Kristine. You and I have come a long way in our
friendship, and I also feel the friendship is stronger
now, too.*

*I think we will always have those dreadful memories
of the past, but we will also always remember that we
still have each other. I am so proud of the woman you
were and are. I never doubted you as a person, but I
am so thankful that you did not let this rape change
you for the worse. I respect you so much, and it makes
me happy to see you so happy now. All I wanted for
you was happiness, and it makes me feel some sense
of resolution seeing you with JR. He has made you
trust the male sex again. He is the light at the end of
the tunnel, and I truly feel JR symbolizes what all of
us wanted for you: happiness, love, respect, trust, and
faith.*

*I still remember the past, but I am so proud of your fu-
ture. I feel you will always have this scar as a reminder of your past, but you will always have your family*

*and friends as a constant reminder that you are not
that person anymore.*

MOM AND DAD IRWIN

Two people who didn't know me at the time of the rape, J.R.'s
parents, are still affected by my rape. I'm so grateful to these
two people who have embraced me and loved me just as I am.

MOM IRWIN

*First let me say that I think you are an amazing per-
son. Maybe even the nicest person I have ever met.
How anyone could deliberately hurt you is beyond my
understanding. Given the chance to select a wife for
JR, and another daughter for me, I never for a second
looked beyond you. You are very special to me and I
am proud to have you as my daughter. I love you very
much.*

*As far as your rape, it has made you who you are. By
making you the fighter on one side and kind hearted to
all people on the other. We can't change what happened to you but we can learn. You have grown into a
strong wonderful person.*

*When talking about rape in general, I believe that
many people fault the person who was raped.
Wrong...but they do. Your helping others in this position is a testament to who you are. I am very proud of
you.*

DAD IRWIN

*The word "daughter" has a very special meaning to
me. I had two daughters in my life before J.R. introduced you into my life, and wasn't sure how I would
feel about having someone else call me "Dad" and
having a another "daughter" in my life.*

I know the answer; it is wonderful!!! You are a marvelously strong, intelligent and above all, loving and caring person who am proud to call my daughter and even prouder to have you call me Dad. I love you with all of my heart and thank you for bringing such happiness to my son's life. If God had given me the right to design a perfect wife for my son, I could not have designed a more perfect one. And when I say perfect, I mean perfect.

There is a song out currently (I can't remember the name) that has a lyric where they say, "perfect in your imperfections."

I wish more people would listen to those lyrics. To me, it doesn't mean we can't have done anything wrong or had anything wrong happen to us. It meant that we are loved and love ourselves without the need to be "perfect."

You know that I deal with broken marriages and families on a daily basis and have for 37+ years. I have heard some horrible stories of sexual abuse and rape. I have seen women, and in some cases boys and girls, who have carried a burden in their hearts and minds that they had no part in creating.

I have never distinguished or differentiated rape between sexual abuse. To me they are both horrendous.

Having said all of that, I can say that in those 37+ years I have also seen the destruction and devastation that these acts have caused to their innocent victims. In some cases the cost has been a person's life.

That is why I am so very, very proud of you. It may seem trite, but you took lemons and made lemonade from them. You met this crime head on and became a stronger person because of it.

My chest puffs out with pride when I think about the women you have already helped by sharing your story and all of the others you will help in the future.

I love you and I am very proud of you!!

CHAPTER 6

It May Seem I Have the Happy Ending—But It's More Complicated than That

IN JANUARY 2015, JR AND I FOUND OUT we were having a little boy. I was excited, but scared. I didn't know anything about boys, and I wondered if I was capable enough to raise a boy. I immediately felt the burden of teaching our son—still a fetus in the womb—the concepts of consent and respect. I wondered if I could, and when, I should tell him what had happened to me. It felt almost as if receiving the responsibility to raise a boy in this world was a test. My joy and anticipation was all mixed up with this worry.

Our son, James, whom we call Jay, was born two days after my birthday on June 4, 2015. As soon as that boy came into my arms, I knew he was an amazing gift from God, and I could do this. I could be a great mom but also teach Jay how *people*, not just women, should be treated.

During my maternity leave, I became convinced that I needed to step up my advocacy to be a role model for my son. How was I to do that? It had been eight years since the rape, and

82   VOICES OF HOPE
    One Rape Survivor Plus Her Family & Friends
    Share Their Empowering Road to Recovery

I had done some speaking engagements, although not that many. Fortunately, I had given enough presentations to give me some credibility as a speaker. I was also working on my "letter" project, which I knew I wanted eventually to develop into some form of a book. At the time, I still didn't have enough letters to turn my book idea into a reality.

It had been over a year-and-a-half since I had started sending out the letters. I kept all of the responses together, but I didn't read any of them. I wanted to wait because I knew reading the letters would bring up a lot of emotion. I also didn't know how to proceed.

My mom introduced me to Beth Caldwell, a speaker, author, and founder of Pittsburgh Professional Women and The Leadership Academy. We decided to meet for lunch. I remember sitting there with my two-month-old son and my mother, explaining my thought process on the letters to Beth. She provided insight and inspiration on what to do and how to get this project going as a book. She also recommended that I gain more speaking engagements. I left that meeting feeling empowered.

By the end of August, I had secured three speaking engagements for September: Pittsburgh's Action against Rape (PAAR) recommended me for an event called Walk a Mile in Her Shoes®; the University of Pittsburgh invited me to speak at their event called Undy Run; and Bowling Green State University invited me to speak to kick off their October program.

Now I had three upcoming speaking engagements, and I felt unprepared. In the past, I had just gotten up and told my story; I didn't really prepare, I just spoke. I had thought that a spontaneous presentation would feel more real to the audience; but now it felt jumbled. I worried that I might forget something. So, I reached out to Bonnie Budzowski, a presentation and book coach that Beth had recommended. Bonnie and I sat down and discussed my presentation. Bonnie helped me organize my presentation in a way that was easy for the listener to understand, but also clearly delivered my points. With this newly-structured presentation, I was able to tell my story and more. I was able to deliver a message about how to prevent a rape from happening to you, the positive role friends can play in protecting each other, and where to get help if you are a victim.

A fellow survivor organized a local version of the first event, Walk a Mile in Her Shoes®. Walk a Mile is an international organization providing the opportunity for men to raise awareness in their communities about the serious causes, effects, and remediation to men's sexualized violence against women. It was wonderful to give my new presentation at this event.

The second event was the University of Pittsburgh's Undy Run. Fifty participants ran to stress the fact that even if a woman dresses in undergarments, she is not asking to be raped.

At the last engagement, at Bowling Green State University, I was able to show part of my *Fighter* video, which was eye opening for members of the audience.

At about this same time, I turned my letter project toward social media. Over the previous few months, Julie and I had been having endless discussions over what to call my letter project. We considered Secondary Victims, or Secondhand Victims. Ultimately, we decided on Voices of Hope.

I felt this name was most appropriate for several reasons. First, all of these letters represent voices—voices that want to be heard—voices that want to shed some light on what they have gone through. Second, the letters represent voices of hope because they can help someone else who may know a friend who has been a victim. Third, my mom runs a nonprofit called Wings of Hope, and I thought this name was a good fit for my family.

As I said, I took my project to social media not only to support my speaking engagements, but also to engage in a conversation around sexual violence. I began to post news articles of current events and write blog posts to share. I invite you to visit me at https://www.voices-of-hope.org/social-media.

Once September was past, I slowed down a bit on the speaking front, but continued to look for opportunities to speak.

In the coming months, I was invited back to the University of Pittsburgh to speak in February at their "It's on US" chain reveal. For this event, students signed a link to a chain, and then organizers hung the chain so everyone could see who supported the event. It was inspiring to see so many people acknowledge the fact that it is everyone's responsibility to stop sexual violence.

For April 2016, Sexual Assault Awareness Month, I had a speaking engagement lined up for each week. On top of that, I participated in Red My Lips, wearing red lipstick every day this time. I was able to get some relatives to join in on the movement, which was extremely powerful.

With work, all the events going on around Voices of Hope, and my family life, April flew by. Also, on the back end, I began officially working on the book. I always thought I'd write the book quickly, but sometimes the words didn't come easily. The process took much longer than I had anticipated.

In June, I spoke at PAAR's annual golf outing in June. This would be my last speaking engagement for a while, as I needed a break. The weekend before the speaking event was Jay's first birthday party, and then two days after the speaking event, JR and I took a vacation to Nashville.

During that time, another idea that I had been tossing around started to become clear. I called it The Consent Coaster Campaign. I designed coasters to distribute to bars and restaurants throughout the month of April of the following year to start conversations on consent and sexual violence.

That year, I was chosen as one of *Pittsburgh Magazine's* "40 Under 40" award recipients. I couldn't believe I had made the list. It was truly an honor, but it was also scary. I remember getting the call from one of the writers from the magazine about my story. Those who had nominated me had submitted their version of my story and shared that I ran Voices of Hope. The writer wanted to ensure that my story was presented in the way I wanted.

After we went over the story, the reporter asked me a question: "What is something that people don't know about you?" I said that I got to meet Britney Spears and that it was a childhood dream. After I hung up the phone, I thought to myself, "Really? *Really*, Kristine? That is the best you could come up with? You couldn't have said, 'Oh I ran four half marathons,' or 'I hate the sound of Velcro®.'"

Then I thought, "You know what? That is a part of me. I love Britney, and whoever judges me because of it, well it doesn't matter." Of course, Lady Gaga was mentioned in the "40 Under 40" article, too.

I remember the day I was to get my picture taken for the "40 Under 40" magazine piece. I took the day off from work, and I had someone do my makeup professionally. Before I went to get my makeup done, anxiety began to kick in. This was scary. I felt scared because the magazine, award, and event represent a different way that I am sharing my story. I am used to standing in front of a group of people and talking about what happened and what I have learned, but this was different.

My story was going to be in *Pittsburgh Magazine* and widely distributed. This was out of my comfort zone. When I go to speaking engagements, most likely the people who choose to attend are not blaming me. Yet, because of the stigma our culture has on the topic, rape victims are still blamed. Now my story was going out to the public, outside of that safe zone of my speaking engagements. When I got in the car and turned on the radio, the song *Just Dance* by Lady Gaga came on. In my mind, I immediately went to all of the Gaga shows I had been to. I thought about how free I felt in those concerts and about how telling my story helps me break the chains that the rape uses to drag me down. I was okay then. I could do this.

The week of the awards, my company sent out a mass e-mail that had the "40 Under 40" article in it. I received some e-mails from colleagues, congratulating me and telling me how inspired they are by me. I am very humbled that people think that I am inspiring; but my response to everyone who congratulated me was the same:

> *I am truly honored to have this award, but this isn't*
> *about me getting recognized. It is about all those indi-*
> *viduals who have had to suffer from this form of vio-*
> *lence. I hope that by being vocal, I can help the heal-*
> *ing in others. I want to help others find their own*
> *voices.*

The day of the awards ceremony was surreal. Much of it is a blur in my memory. When I was leaving the actual ceremony, two rape survivors stopped and thanked me for the work that I do. They are the reason I do what I do.

I do what I do because I want to help the voiceless find a voice. I want people to know they are not alone. Those who come up to me after presentations are the true ones who inspire me, not myself. Because I tell my story, I am sometimes the first person a survivor tells about his or her rape. That's a *huge* weight off a survivor's shoulders. It's a new step toward healing, and it's worth every effort I make. When survivors stand together and tell their stories, we heal. When we all have conversations about rape, culture, and blame, we create a better world.

* * * * * *

Looking back over the 10-plus years since my rape, I can see the healing path and the grace of God in my story. Sometimes it seems that I ultimately got the fairy tale ending that every woman dreams of—the story I used to dream of. I have never been in love with anyone the way I'm in love with my husband, and I had no idea I could love another human being the way that I love my son.

As I was finishing this book we learned we were having another child. I just had a feeling the baby was a boy, even though I had dreamt about my deceased grandmother coming back to tell me I was having a girl. At our first sonogram, the technician walked us through each image of the baby. She then asked, "Okay, do you want to know the sex?" JR and I both said, "Yes." She said, "It's a girl!"

I was floored because I was totally expecting a boy. We had some names picked for a girl, but we weren't set just yet, and I had no ideas for decorating a nursery for a girl. But, of course, names and decorations weren't my biggest concerns.

I wondered how I would present what had happened to me to my daughter. Would it be same way I tell my son, Jay? How would I teach my daughter about sexual violence and how to respect people in general?

The more I thought about it, the more I became convinced that I should teach both of my children in the same way. I will tell both of my children what happened to me, when I feel I am ready, and I will teach them both about consent, bystander intervention, and respecting people. Sexual violence isn't a gender-related act of violence, and I should not teach my son any differently than I teach my daughter.

I am also convinced that, as JR and I are strong individuals, both Jay and Zella, who was born on October 20th, 2017, are going to be strong individuals who make the world a better place.

While I feel truly blessed, I don't want to leave you with the wrong impression. Some moments aren't so happy. I still have triggering moments; I still have thoughts that scare the shit out of me. These things don't destroy my happiness, but I still have to deal with them. While my rape experience doesn't define me, it will always be a part of who I am. Even in the best of outcomes, rape leaves a lifetime wound.

For years, I hated the smell of fall, and it took some time to realize that this makes sense. On a chilly October night, somewhere in the woods, I was violated. I am sure I was on the ground in the dirt and leaves, and that the scent of fall made an impression on my brain. Only after I met JR did I begin to learn to control my aversion to this smell. Sometimes, fall still bothers me, but not as much as in the past. The strength of the trigger decreases as the years go on, but it is still there.

I can't begin to explain how many hours and days I have spent contemplating the character of my perpetrator. For a reason I don't understand, I sometimes still struggle to know if he was a good person or not. I also want to know how I could have trusted him. My perpetrator was not a stranger; he was someone I had worked with at the convenience store all summer. Why would someone I knew and trusted want to do this to me?

I have researched my perpetrator repeatedly, just in hopes of finding something. But what *is* that something I'm looking for? I don't know. I've looked for some kind of clue regarding what made this happen. Was it an accident? I know, of course, that you don't rape someone by accident, but these thoughts have run through my mind.

Recently, while driving home one night from work, I was surprised by a vision of the rape itself. I don't remember the rape, but my mind was struggling to remember or visualize it all these years later. It was disgusting and uncomfortable. I had to find a way to get that image out of my mind because it makes me cringe just writing about it.

The frequency and violence of rape can still catch me off guard. Recently, at a candlelight vigil for survivors, a group of performers put on a dance called *1 in 5* to symbolize the statistic that one in five women will get raped in her lifetime. Standing there watching with my friend Julie, I began to feel as if a heavy weight were on my chest and I had difficulty breathing. Watching this fact about rape being acted out in a form that I had never seen before was scary.

At speaking engagements, I mostly feel safe, but sometimes I get fearful that someone in the audience might know my perpetrator and realize I was his victim. I become frightened that person will hurt me. And as I said above, telling my story in new ways, such as the exposure that came with "40 Under 40," can bring me intense anxiety. It was scary to think that all the people reading that magazine might be judging me deciding that my rape was my fault.

This fear of being blamed haunts me sometimes. Our society is quick to blame victims, and it's been a struggle not to blame myself. I left with my perpetrator alone; I drank too much; I put myself in a dangerous situation. So, it is difficult not to blame myself.

Now as a parent, I get even more frightened. I hope that I can raise mu children to truly understand what respect is and how to intervene as a bystander when something isn't right. I cry when I read stories of how children are victimized. I cry because I do not want something like this happening my son, my daughter, or any other child.

With all of these feelings, I feel I have a huge responsibility to reach out to others and teach them about respect, consent, bystander intervention, and sexual violence. I have been able to heal to a large extent, but the need to continue healing is a part of who I am. I have good days and bad days, but I still have to find ways to get past the moments that trigger my dark thoughts. My deepest hope is that by reaching out and engaging others, I can help myself and others to find the power to heal. I hope I can help those who have not experienced this form of violence to realize what an issue this is.

Sometimes I think back to my favorite Disney princess, Ariel. The beautiful mermaid traded her voice for human legs. She lost her voice and had to fight to get it back. In that process, she was able to fall in love, and her prince accepted her for everything she is and was.

I feel that Ariel's story connects with mine because I lost so much due to my rape. I've struggled, and sometimes continue to struggle, to find my self-esteem, my sense of security, and control. I've worked hard to find my voice so that I can share my story with others. Like Ariel, I need to be loved for who I am and who I was—broken history and current struggles alike. JR, my prince, is wonderful, but we all need more than one person.

Even the best prince can't undo the past, and none of us can guarantee that a prince will come into our lives, anyway. We can, however, extend ourselves as a community of love and acceptance. As survivors, family members, and friends, we can bring healing to each other.

This leads me to reach out directly to you. Yes, you, the one reading. I hope that as you finish reading this book, you have a better sense of understanding of rape and the issues surrounding it. I hope you can see how everyone reacts differently and needs space and love. I hope you learned that everyone, including friends and family, is affected. The destruction and pain of rape extends beyond the physical victim.

I urge you to take a stance and realize that sexual violence is serious. This is no light matter. Stop any rape jokes; stop blaming the victims; and start educating yourself on the issue. If you know someone who has been a victim, listen, but don't force.

If you have experienced this form of violence, I hope you find the power to reclaim your life and call it your own. If you have never gone through anything like this, please be aware that people around you have. Take the time to learn more and stand up for what is right.

Now is the time to bring sexual violence to a halt. It isn't going to happen overnight, but with each person "being a voice" for another, we can make a difference and change our culture's view on rape. This responsibility belongs to all of us.

Thanks, *Kristine*